NEW WINESKINS

New Wineskins

A plea for radical rethinking in the Church of England to enable normal church growth to take effect beyond existing parish boundaries

David Pytches

Brian Skinner

EAGLE
Guildford, Surrey

ISBN 0–86347–029–7

Published by Eagle, an imprint of Inter Publishing Service
(IPS) Ltd, Williams Building, Woodbridge Meadows,
Guidford GU1 1BH.
Set in New Century Schoolbook by Watermark, Cromer,
Norfolk, NR27 9HL.
Printed in Great Britain by William Collins Ltd, Glasgow.

Contents

Foreward   xi
1   Parish Boundaries Questioned   13
2   Need for Parallel Structures   23
3   Issues of Ecclesiology   29
4   Precedents for Flexibility   37
5   Dynamics in Church Growth   49
6   The Way Ahead   57
    Appendix A: St John's, Downshire Hill, Hampstead   61
    Appendix B: The Church on the Bridge   63
    Appendix C: The Fellowship of the King, Bristol
        Stephen Abbott   65
    Appendix D: Local Community Churches in
        Chester-le-Street   Ian Bunting   71
    Appendix E: Mobile 'Seed' Teams and Cross Cultural
        Planting   Robert Gardner-Hopkins   79
    Appendix F: Limits to Growth Within the Parish
        Charlie Cleverly   91
    Appendix G: The Dilemma Facing a Growing Church
        David Huggett   97

'I look upon the world as my parish.'

John Wesley
(*Journal*, 11 June, 1739)

Acknowledgements

The authors wish to express their most sincere thanks to Canon
John Tiller for his challenging foreword and to the following, who
have read the manuscript and offered us their helpful criticisms
and constructive suggestions:

The Rt Rev. Colin Buchanan
The Rev. Dr Christopher Cocksworth
The Rev. Dr Eddie Gibbs
The Rev. Principal David Gillett
The Rt Rev. Patrick Harris
The Rev. Bob Gardner-Hopkins
The Rev. Teddy Saunders
The Rev. Dr Nigel Scotland
The Rev. Canon Robert Warren

Also to the following who have contributed most useful case his-
tories detailed in the appendices:

The Rev. Stephen Abbott
The Rev. Ian Bunting
The Rev. Charlie Cleverly
The Rev. Bob Gardner-Hopkins
The Rev. David Huggett

The final responsibility for what is produced here is, of course,
ours.

David Pytches
Brian Skinner

Foreword

This little 'tract for the times' should be read by bishops, members of the General Synod, and all others in positions of leadership and influence in the Church of England, and perhaps especially by archdeacons and those who are involved in the appointment of incumbents.

The argument may be criticised on many points of detail. It is admitted on page 47 that the book has been hastily researched, and this shows. The authors say that they are 'obviously' committed to the unity of the Church, but they recommend that congregations which cannot get on together should split up. Church growth is understood in numerical terms alone, and the New Testament concept of spiritual growth being about learning to worship and witness together as men and women who do not choose each other but are chosen by God, is replaced by open advocacy that we should choose the church which suits us best.

If I don't go along with the authors in much of what they say, why do I urge people to read their work? For two reasons. The first is that they make it crystal clear that the parochial system should be about the living witness of the local church, and not about defining 'cures for souls' for individual clergymen who then become entrenched behind boundaries where they are secure in their rights to operate a spiritual 'closed shop' as far as the Church of England is concerned.

The second reason is that the urgent demands of mission to our country require the Church to employ many different kinds of outreach structures apart from the purely geographical ones. Something in the way of networks of basic Christian communities is needed to sustain these different kinds of mission and this book illustrates well some of the ways in which this can happen. The Church of England has got to be flexible enough to embrace and encourage these alternatives to the parochial system if it is going to have any kind of significant place in the future spiritual life of our nation. That is the point on which the authors have a burning conviction, and I agree with them.

Canon John Tiller, Hereford Cathedral

1

Parish Boundaries Questioned

The parish system is not without its positive benefits in certain circumstances – it has, for example, helped some urban churches to keep their congregations at a time when the tendency has been to move out to the suburbs (sometimes compared to 'white flight' in the USA). However, it is a system originally designed to meet the pastoral needs of a 'Christian' country. Today the parish system seriously inhibits the renewal and growth of the Church of England. The model is too static and hinders growth for many active churches. It shuts off vast parts of the country from effective outreach, thereby making it more difficult for the Anglican Church to fulfil its role as the Church of the Nation.

We now live in a secular post-Christian country. There are already signs of 'religious' awakening, but the Church of England will fail to maximise on this if the traditional assumptions of the parish system are rigidly adhered to.

Whilst not necessarily rejecting the concept of a parish for some purposes we wish to indicate the inappropriateness of key aspects of the system with the following observations and reservations.

1 The Church of England clearly embraces many different expressions of worship and church life. No single pattern suits everybody, but any one local

church can only express its own particular style and ethos. This inevitably leaves a number of Anglicans in any given area without a local expression of Anglican Church life which suits their own expectations and needs.

It is an attractive feature of the Church of England that it has plenty of intellectual space within which to move and is tolerant of a wide diversity of sincerely held, but differing, expressions of the Christian faith. Whilst insisting on the centrality of Christ and the statements in the Creed, the Church of England leaves ample scope for individual Anglicans, clergy and parish churches to interpret 'secondary issues' in a variety of ways.

Paul Avis ably reinforces this latter point by reminding us that from the Reformation to at least the rise of the Tractarian Movement, Anglicanism regarded matters of church government and order as secondary issues, ie: *adiaphora* (lit) 'things indifferent'. (*Anglicanism and the Christian Church*, 1989, Edinburgh, T&T Clark)

2   Those Anglicans in any parish, who do not find the local parish church style appropriate to their own conviction or personality, are at present obliged to attend another denominational/non-denominational church within their parish or, if wanting to remain loyal Anglicans, to find some neighbouring or distant parish church which suits them.

'The exercise of choice and mobility are characteristics of the urban mentality/culture' (Dr Eddie Gibbs).

3   The challenge of the gospel, and the need in our country, is for Christians to witness evangelistically to those with whom they have contact – including, most naturally, those in their own business and social circles

as well as in their own neighbourhoods. Recognition of this will become particularly significant as we enter the 'Decade of Evangelism'.

4 One of the New Testament characteristics of church life was that of local identity. This is also a particular need in our culture today, where so much else appears to be rootless and transient.

5 When Anglicans who feel unable to attend their local parish church influence their neighbours for Christ, it is natural, but not satisfactory, that they will take these people to their own regular place of worship – outside their locality. Where else would they encourage them to go?

6 The number of people who can be effectively influenced in a meaningful and personal way by any one individual clergyman is very limited. Certainly it is much smaller than the average population of an English parish. It is quite impossible to imagine that a local vicar is going to be able to 'reach' all of his parish.
   Whilst the parish system gives the incumbent the 'cure of the souls' in his parish, it limits the 'cure' to those under his authority and leadership, even where he may have neither the inclination nor the ability to plan and work for it. In any case, many of his 'souls' will be outside the parish for the main part of the week. They may well meet more people outside their own parish than within it.

7 This has highlighted the need to release the laity into their proper New Testament role of active participation in the ministry of their local church. Happily, the vital function of the laity in ministry has been taught and encouraged   in   some   parts   of   the   Church   of

England for many years. But if these lay people have an Anglican allegiance outside their own parish church, the assumptions of the parish system inhibit the potential for growth and consolidation from their contacts. This is often the case where active churches have relatively inactive or unevangelistic churches in adjacent areas.

8   Churches grow as the Holy Spirit uses the gifts and leadership skills of particular individuals, through their circle of contacts. The ownership of a particular building for worship, or the existence of an administrative structure, does not ensure that the church's outreach will be permanent. The church, as the people of God in a given area, may thrive for a time and then decline for a variety of reasons. We need to incorporate that expectation into our patterns of church life.

9   The work of the Holy Spirit in building Christ's Church is not only dynamic, but organic – church growth cannot be brought about simply by our planning or the endeavours of church bureaucrats. We must follow where we believe the Holy Spirit is leading. We cannot restrain and restrict him by parish boundaries.

The parish system implies a permanence and rigidity which is no longer suitable to our needs; parochial boundaries in some places today are as irrelevant as the Berlin Wall.

10   Where the church of a geographically small parish is filled to overflowing (and there is no obvious possibility of further growth) should it settle for 'plateauing' at some maximum size, lest it spill over parish boundaries, or should it plan for church growth and church planting?

'The time may have come to revise our understanding of what constitutes a "parish" and to define it as a congregation or set of congregations, rather than as a geographical area. Lines on maps sometimes bear little relation to patterns of actual Christian community.' (*Plan for Evangelism and Church Growth in the Diocese of Wellington*, New Zealand, 1988, p. 14)

Why should God's church continue to be organised in a way that effectively 'protects' many people from the impact of the Gospel?

This is the case in those parishes where the local parish church has little or no vision for outreach, or where the numbers of residents in the parish are too many to be reached by the committed members of that church. Very often this may simply reflect the fact that the particular style of their church is failing to cut much ice in its own area.

There should at least be both freedom and encouragement for others to do this outreach – and to do it as part of an Anglican network, rather than oblige such growth to be cut off from the 'Church of the Nation'. (See J. Moltmann's chapter on the subject in *The Church and the Power of the Holy Spirit*, (SCM, 1979) where Moltmann argues for double strategies and parallel ecclesiologies. He sees this as the historical reality of the church of Jesus Christ.)

What is needed is to break down the mentality that adheres to the belief that the parish priest has the ownership rights of the spiritual needs of people living within any particular area. The Free Churches have already shown us that parallel structures for Christian worship and ministry can operate without necessarily damaging the life of the 'parish' church in the locality.

It is true that there may be certain tensions arising from competition, or at least comparison. But is that necessarily bad? God has made us all very different and, as we have said, no one style is going to suit everybody. Let us diversify our appeal (even as Anglicans) and thereby reach more for Christ.

It may be argued that a larger and growing church should ask some of its members to leave and join nearby struggling churches desperately in need of encouragement. Whilst it is expected that they would receive every encouragement from their 'sending' leadership if they so chose to go (occasionally it has happened to our knowledge, and certainly we have tried this from St Andrews, Chorleywood), the reality is that it does not happen on a sufficient scale and when it does there are too often so many problems involved that the experiment comes to nought. It would not be appropriate to cite specific instances, but rather we wish to acknowledge the reality of failure despite the best of intentions.

The struggling church may be viewed by the members so sent as a 'hard missionary challenge' or even 'a lost cause' and the receiving church may not welcome the particular style or evangelistic emphasis of those coming from the 'sending' church. The transferred member(s) may find that the leadership of the 'receiving' church does not really share the same vision which motivated the one(s) 'sent'.

In some circumstances there seems to be a clear indication that what is needed is an alternative structure – a new wineskin. This would allow members of a church who live outside the boundaries of their parish to develop naturally in their own area and to be accepted as the legitimate nucleus of a new church structure, whilst still retaining links with the original 'mother' church. This would keep the lines open for a wholesome relationship with the wider church.

Undoubtedly, one of the concerns in considering this is the effect that outreach to a neighbouring parish may have on the Anglican church in whose parish it is. This church may already feel it has its back to the wall and be trying desperately to hold together a wide variety of expectations within its existing congregation.

An alternative 'wineskin' that has overspilt into an adjacent parish might tend to drain off a number from the congregation of that neighbouring parish church, but this is an ongoing process. However, loss as a result of disaffection is a constant danger to every congregation whether or not there is another Anglican fellowship nearby.

This concern highlights the need to proceed in a spirit of true Christian love and mutual respect and an atmosphere of openness and good communication, though it must not be assumed that no move can ever be made without the full approval of neighbouring congregations, who may feel themselves threatened by any change. The primary concern throughout must be for evangelistic outreach particularly as we launch the Decade of Evangelism. An alternative wineskin may relieve some of the pressure on those clergymen who are sincerely trying to provide too inclusive a menu for all sorts and tastes, simply because they see themselves as the only church serving the parish. They may be able to reach others more effectively by sharpening the focus on their own particular emphases and calling.

A loosening up of attitudes, encouraged from above by our diocesan bishops, could release a fresh opportunity for renewal in the life of the whole Church. There should be nothing in this which contravenes the fundamental statutory requirements of a New Testament church, although we recognise that some traditional Anglican assumptions would inevitably be questioned by such a relaxation.

This questioning process is an essential activity and never more necessary than when it concerns the structures for new life in our own mainline catholic Church, which has been re-shaped in the upheaval of the

Reformation, invigorated by the Wesleyan revival, influenced by the Tractarian movement and, more recently, able to contemplate measures which would have been generally considered impossible fifty years ago, that is, the ordination of women and divorcees, even at the expense of scandalising some other main line churches and many of its own members also.

The parish system is neither sacrosanct nor carved in stone. Since the late 1950s it has been seriously challenged for its inappropriateness as a matrix for church growth. It was never a part of British church life before Theodore of Tarsus, the then Archbishop of Canterbury, who laid the foundations for it between the years AD 669–690. This was an imposed transplant, originally taken over from the administrative divisions of the Roman Empire. Diocesan bishops replaced the roving missionary-type bishop of the Celtic church and monastic systems operated as outposts for evangelism.

Parish boundaries must be seen as transient structures, which admirably suited the needs of a previous age, but in many if not most places actually inhibit the life of the church today. It must, therefore, come as a considerable surprise to any newcomer to our denomination to see how restrictive and inhibiting the parish system is to the natural numerical growth and renewal of our church. The Tiller Report refers to the parochial system as 'a weak instrument for mission' (p. 72ff). We can regard it as the condom of the Church of England!

The traditional Anglican ambivalence to the *adiaphora* is the real point at issue here. Paul Avis (*Anglicanism and the Christian Church*, 1989, Edinburgh, T&T Clark) shows how the *adiaphora* was seen by the main line Reformers (Continental as well as English) as including matters of order. This was taken up and developed, particularly in Anglicanism, by Hooker and others, who sharply distinguished between doctrine and polity. They saw polity as belonging to the realm of adiaphora and, therefore, not deriving in some immutable way from Scripture, but as dependent on all sorts of pragmatic concerns.

A softening of attitudes and some initial changes in expectations today regarding parish boundaries could release a lot of new spiritual energy within the land. It is, however, recognised that there are all sorts of other issues and questions which would soon surface once the flood gates were burst open, particularly issues of ministry and training, the nature and use of the sacraments, etc., and even the establishment of the Church of England itself. The prospect is so overwhelming that it would seem impossible to proceed. But it is possible – it is beginning to happen! We must trust the Holy Spirit and not demand to know exactly how things will develop if some parish boundaries are relaxed. We quote, with strong approval, Peter Norvic's courageous comments about boundaries:

> There is often great resistance to changing boundaries, mainly because we have got used to living and working with a certain group of people and we like it that way. But, if the interests of mission are to have priority, then we must be prepared to be unsentimental about...boundaries. These are matters about which feelings often run high and in which we spend a great deal of time and energy in debate and argument.... Boundaries are very secondary considerations and should be dealt with decisively and without too much wasteful debate. (*Moving Forward: A Strategy for the Diocese of Norwich* the Bishop of Norwich, 1989, p. 12)

Once we can accept the possibility that parish boundaries are in fact inhibiting church growth, we may tentatively start to look around for some more viable structure to suit the current needs of the church.

It is a mistake to regard the local church simply as an

administrative area, like a secular parish. A congregation does not consist simply of those who live within a boundary. The local church, when it is dispersed, is a network of relating Christians, who straggle out across communities acting as salt and light in the world.

The Rev. Charlie Cleverley suggests that if we are to take the Decade of Evangelism seriously, then we should ignore parish boundaries completely for the time being and evaluate them again in the year 2,000 to see if the system is then worth restoring (see his book *Church Planting*, to be published by Scripture Union in 1991).

The church is rightly beginning to emphasise evangelism during the coming decade. Many programmes and suggestions are being mooted and no doubt many successful evangelistic campaigns will be conducted. However, we have so far to hear of any reference at all to church planting, which must be a *sine qua non* to genuine evangelism. We do not believe that enough thought is being given to this by the Anglican Church – at all levels.

Our proposal is that when a church is found to be growing in a given locality, that it be encouraged to develop separate 'new wineskins' – to found new centres of worship, to create new congregations, even if this means going beyond traditional parish boundaries and establishing such a 'wineskin' in another parish.

2

Need for Parallel Structures

Plea for 'New Wineskins'

For some time we have been hearing prophecies that a Christian revival is coming to Britain and we believe them. We have prayed for revival. We have experienced revivals several times in this nation in the past. We are seeing revival happening in many other parts of the world today. The moral climate is certainly ripe for it in Britain at this time and it must be something that God wants so much to send to his Church.

Yet how would our average churches cope with thousands of new members coming in, who were from the ranks of the completely unchurched. They would undoubtedly experience a number of culture shocks:

1   They would find traditional forms of worship, religious language, and dress (not just the clergy, but even the laity) irrelevant.

2   They would find the traditional style of leadership inflexible.

3   They would find the architectural ethos of most churches and the seating in pews inappropriate, uncomfortable and inconvenient.

23

4   They would find the plethora of books in the pew –
Bible, Prayer Book, hymn books, booklets, cards and
notice sheets – incomprehensible.

5   They would find the restrictions of existing parish
boundaries frustrating. Why not simply go to the
nearest church, rather than travel miles to the one
with the 'right' blend, the one to which they were originally introduced. They would also find the size of many
growing churches forbidding. The natural expression of
the living church is to birth daughter churches by
dividing off into smaller local regroupings.

6   Most potential leaders would find the problems of
their own ordination into leadership within the Anglican Church insurmountable.

7   They would find the burden of guilt imposed upon
them for the disorder created through their inclusion
into the local church intolerable.

Jesus refers to the traditional structures as old wineskins. It seems from his teaching on this subject (see Luke
5:36–39) that we should bear in mind that none of these
things associated with the old structures is necessarily
wrong. Neither are they without value nor meaningless
even though for many people they may be irrelevant,
inappropriate and intolerable. Those of us who were
brought up in these ways still find many of them very helpful. Many of those who worship God in Anglican churches
today still feel very much at home in their old wineskins.

But, not surprisingly, the old wine feels very
threatened by the new wine because, as Jesus says, the
new wine will burst the old wineskins and the old wine
will be lost, as indeed will be the new wine also. The revival would come and go and no one would seem to be any

the better for it – in fact things could even be the worse for a divine visitation! New wine with all its fizz can be very threatening stuff indeed!

We are conscious that we are overlooking the possibility of some old wineskins becoming sufficiently flexible to retain the new wine. There are too few examples of this to justify the hope that the spiritual needs of our land will be met adequately in this way.

In proceeding, we must respect the old wineskins, and love the old wine which some say is better (Luke 5:39). But let us seek to persuade those who are used to the old structures to see the need for new wineskins, to help constructively and sacrificially towards their creation; indeed, in every way to bless the new wineskins and the new wine. In previous times the creation of new wine skins has too often been achieved through a spirit of rebellion and not under the direction of the Holy Spirit.

We believe that those churches which can bless the new wine skins will be blessed themselves – this way some of the fizz might even penetrate the old wineskins in a beneficial way through the process of osmosis. Though not necessarily on Anglican church premises, this way the new wineskins will be 'Anglican-friendly' from the start. Some may fall into heresy or simply die. Others in time may come into a more identifiable Anglican order or merge with a nearby Baptist church or perhaps link up with a network of 'House churches'.

Whatever fountains of life were in the original new wineskins will flow on into the mainstream of God's catholic church in due time (and by that time it may no longer be anything like a recognisable orthodox Anglican church).

We have to be ready to let these things happen. All this will seem rather untidy to our western minds, but it is a natural way for churches to grow. We witnessed this first hand in South America in the sixties, seventies and eighties.

The life must come first. The church order develops later. There was apparently quite a lot of church life going on in Crete before Paul sent Titus along to tidy things up by ordaining elders in the churches there. There is plenty of precedent in Britain's ecclesiastical history for permitting alternative wineskins beyond the local parish setting. (Canonical authority for this could be found under Canon B 41.)

The question may be asked: 'What, then, would a new wineskin look like?'

We cannot say exactly any more than we can say exactly who an expected baby will look like at birth. It would simply be a tiny new human being. It might not be really identifiable with either father or mother.

But as we prepare for the new wine we can study the varieties of existing wineskins, especially some of the newer ones. We can identify and evaluate the structures for developing order and maintaining truth. We can stress the essential place of the Word of God and the Sacraments, though exactly who ministers the Word and/or the Sacraments can be left open for the time being (we are talking here of ordination to office. Character and maturity in leadership will always be relevant). We can also seek to identify those tell-tale traits which can so easily cause degeneration into a cult. We can examine the pros and the cons of the exclusive church and the tolerant kind. We shall need to study the relevant biblical principles here and use them to train potential leaders.

In considering leadership within new wineskins we can learn from military strategy: the typical army will aim to train each of its professional soldiers to the level of an NCO, so that when war is declared, and thousands of conscripts called up, leaders are already there to cope with the new intake.

People should be trained at local church level in alternative styles of leadership (NCO's, if you like) for the new wineskins so that when the revival comes a minimal structure will be available which will allow the flexibility necessary to suit the particular needs of the local wineskins.

These wineskins will gradually begin linking up under a larger structure allowing an appropriate leadership to emerge. If the original wineskins are 'Anglican-friendly' from the start (as our proposal intends) the local bishop will have some influence in advising, though initially he would need to be reticent about seeking to impose his authority.

Those chosen to lead will be godly and mature men and women who have recognised gifts of leadership. They will know Jesus as their Lord and Saviour. They will be people of prayer who love the Scriptures. They will be from among those who look to the Holy Spirit to guide them and will be recognised by those around them by his anointing upon their lives for ministry. We can not change the essential faith once entrusted to the saints, but we can change some traditional order where it has become fossilised by the ages. If we search the New Testament afresh we might find that a simple unordained leadership from the locality is all that is required as an adequate minimum (some might believe the ideal) for beginning some of the new local wineskin churches.

3

Issues of Ecclesiology

The nature of the church

Since the New Testament is regarded as our final authority, any definition of the church must focus on our God-
ward relationship through Christ, rather than on any
man-made rules and regulations. Only in this way can we
encompass the whole church rather than 'our' bit of it.
The 'visible' church must allow for the inclusion of all
those who make claim to faith in Christ. When seeking
definitions within the framework of a denomination there
is the constant temptation to limit our idea of the church
to something too domestic and certainly less than the way
God must surely see things. The Church of England still
aspires in some sense to be the 'Church of the Nation' and
this challenges us to promote attitudes and patterns
which are inclusive of the Christian criteria within our
country. We must avoid making walls which will divide
and can only be scaled by the most sophisticated and
traditionally-minded believers. We equally have a
responsibility to minister to the traditionalists and must
not alienate them by appearing to be 'way out' for the
sake of it.

There will, of course, always be those who, by their
own decision, wish to cut themselves off from the
Church of England, but that is a very different matter
from making rules which exclude those who already

have roots in our Church or who wish to be seen to belong.

Any human institution needs to know who its members are. Tangible means of recognition are necessary to identify who belongs and who doesn't. The Church of England has never made very exclusive criteria in this respect. Christian baptism plus parish residence or attendance at an Anglican church is all that is required to get on to an Electoral Roll. This vagueness may well be appropriate, but could surely include those who are active in 'fellowships' which relate to existing Anglican churches. More stringent qualifications may be required of those who are in recognised positions of leadership. The important thing is that the recognition of 'belonging' should not make demands beyond New Testament requirements. Otherwise we deny the true nature of the Church.

From earliest times the people of God have experienced the tension between flexibility and rigidity, between openness to change as they listened to God and their traditions which have become established. The true church includes those who are at both ends of this spectrum and the institution must make every effort to understand and allow scope for both.

The unity of the church

As already expressed, the unity of the church derives from the nature of the church. There can only be one church. Its intrinsic nature is centred in Christ and ultimately he is head of that *one* church. This is the theological reality of love. We must find practical expression of this, rather than simply affirming it – especially when there is so much evidence of division within the 'Body'. On the other hand, the expression of unity must allow for all legitimate variety. Indeed, without variety there would be nothing to unite.

In the Anglican Church, visible unity has commonly focused on the recognised authority of the bishop. Bishops today need to be flexible in the practical out-working of this. Traditionally it has been assumed that a single expression of Anglican style in any given parish is adequate. This may have served well in the past when mobility was more restricted and culture more homogeneous across the nation, but now we live in a mul-ticultural society with an educational system which encourages self-expression and initiative; our society respects variety and the rights of minorities. These and other factors affect people's needs and expectations in church life even when they live in the same area. Nowa-days a single parish may include numerous sub-cultures and the Bishop's oversight should facilitate a variety of Anglican expressions in any given area, rather than inhibit them. This need not militate against unity, pro-vided there is Christian love and mutual respect. We must work for this rather than try to bolster a false sense of spiritual monopoly for the traditional parish priest.

The fellowships proposed here really do not raise theological problems though they may appear radical to the traditional assumptions of parish life. There is bound to be some resistance from local clergy who feel 'threatened' by the possible presence of a parallel Angli-can fellowship in an area hitherto regarded as 'theirs'. If the new work was of some other denomination they would realise there was nothing that they could do about it. Even Jehovah's Witnesses and Muslims become estab-lished in spite of possible antipathy.

Nevertheless patient dialogue must be encouraged. The principles and motivations we have expressed must be clearly presented. It is likely that it will often be neces-sary for the bishop to draw together those affected and help to find mutually acceptable criteria for going for-ward.

If our underlying concern is for the extension of God's Kingdom (or even growth for the wider Anglican Church), we should not worry about alternative emphases around us or even the multiplication of centres of witness and outreach. The marketing principle is worth remembering: 'The greater the number of check-outs the greater the number of people processed.'

The essence of ministry, the place of ordination and the nature of training

During recent years we have come to realise in the Church of England that the 'ministry' is much more than 'ordination'. Whereas the traditionally accepted view is that there are areas of ministry exclusively reserved for the ordained 'priest' – the presidency at the eucharist and the pronouncing of absolution – this has little justification on biblical or theological grounds. Their strongest defence rests on authority and order and cannot be absolute as if it belongs to the 'esse' of the Church. The jurisdiction of the bishop can therefore be used to modify these views if it can be seen that modern circumstances demand it. Increasingly the need for suitable Christians to be recognised and commissioned to minister in all sorts of ways is becoming urgent.

Patterns of training for this ministry still tend to be highly academic and seriously isolated from the evangelistic and pastoral context in which any call is received. Such a system, if persisted with for long, is likely to prove crippling to the existing structures, as was clearly and strongly illustrated by the report *Faith in the City*. The application of the report's recommendations is much wider than its terms of reference, and they should be implemented rapidly. The challenge of the Decade of Evangelism to seek for and expect growth in the church must dictate a bold policy of change in the selection and training of ministers and in the releasing of laity into a fuller share in the ministry of the church. The proper use and purpose of Ordination is for recognition and commissioning of those who reveal in their local and pastoral activities the seal of God's anointing. The present system of training precludes this.

The church needs greater opportunity for those who sense God's call to ordination to test their calling through practical experience of leadership in new centres of witness and worship. On-the-job experience is generally known to be an essential, indeed an indispensable, part of training, and the ability to facilitate growth is one of the truly authentic marks of an effective minister. In practice this has too often been a superficial temporary involvement – ignoring the necessary integral and long term commitment which both produces and sifts out the real potential.

It is expected, therefore, that new church 'fellowships' would be led at their inception by laity, much as home groups are. This would be excellent training, and no context could be more appropriate than the opportunity to play a major role in 'church planting' under the supervision of a responsible mother church. The experience would include working out a strategy for outreach, the pastoring of new converts, the planning of teaching schedules' the 'handling' of social and personal problems and all the regular responsibilities for leadership within the body of Christ, as well as the administration of the Sacraments. It may be that in the present climate an interim procedure for Holy Communion would be to encourage the use of some sort of Agape until the leader is formally ordained. There is no reason why the bishops of our Church could not accept and authorise such a practice. (See *The Case for Lay Presidency* [Grove Booklets] by Alan Hargraves)

The exercise of authority and oversight in the church

As said above, an expression of unity may be seen in the ultimate authority of the bishop, but it is obvious that this authority must be delegated and diffused widely enough for all members of the church to enjoy a sense of loving and effective oversight.

Traditionally, delegation of this authority has been to the parish priest, and sometimes from him to assistant curates, parish workers and other lay helpers at his discretion. More recently the concepts of team and group ministries have allowed for intermediate overseers in the team vicar, etc. Rural deans, archdeacons and others have also played their part. In all these cases delegation (and accountability in the opposite direction) has been within a geographical area for which the 'superior' already has responsibility. This principle needs extending because in reality church growth is essentially based on relationships rather than geographical location. Churches which are growing actively should be encouraged to exercise the oversight from the mother church of new fellowship groups (potential churches) beyond their own area as further outreach takes place. This would still be under the bishop's ultimate authority but intermediate oversight would be needed until the new 'church' was able to stand on its own. It would then relate directly to the bishop or within the local group – whichever is more appropriate.

Church structures

We recognise that new 'church fellowships' will not be modelled exactly on existing parish churches. They will reflect greater simplicity and flexibility. Some may come into being only for a short time and then disappear. This does not necessarily matter. While they exist, they should at least fulfil a worthwhile training function and whatever remains of spiritual value will in some way be caught up in the ever-flowing stream of the life of God's eternal church.

There is no weighty reason why Anglican church life should not include a parallel structure running alongside existing traditional patterns. At times they will overlap and merge while in other cases one may prove to be temporary. In any event, the Church of England needs to acknowledge such changes as make the overall pattern of church life more relevant to the spiritual needs of our changing society.

4

Precedents For Flexibility

One of the arguments often aired by those who do not
wish to consider any change to the present parish system
is that it has worked well historically and continues to
serve the country well, covering every corner. As we are
not arguing for the abolition of the parish system but its
adaptation to current societal trends we will provide in
this chapter many examples, both historical and current,
where the church has shown flexibility in its approach to
particular circumstances.

The most obvious instance of the church working
across parish boundaries is provided by chaplaincies in
hospitals, schools, universities and industry. Further
examples are provided by religious communities, conference centres and the military.

William Grimshaw

One of Wesley's Anglican followers (William Grimshaw
1708–63) was reported to be founding churches in
neighbouring inactive parishes. Complaints were made
to the Archbishop of York (the diocesan bishop), who
defended Grimshaw and rebuked protesting incumbents
for not doing what Grimshaw was doing. Wesley himself
developed a wide open-air ministry by preaching in other
people's parishes' – 'The world is my parish,' he said.

Proprietary chapels

An alternative ordained ministry within a given parish operating under episcopal licence is exemplified in the case of proprietary chapels. These were often built for fashionable preachers by wealthy admirers.

St Mary's, Reading is a proprietary chapel still functioning after two hundred years. The Rev. Dr David Samuel has recently been appointed its minister (November 1990).

There are other similar chapels still operating such as Trinity Church, Buxton in Derbyshire and St Andrew's, Boscombe, Bournemouth. The latter, until recently, had the former Principal of Trinity College, Bristol, the Rev. J. A. Motyer as its minister.

All Saints Church, Sidmouth in Devon, under the incumbancy of the Rev. John Mapson is a kind of proprietary chapel in that there is no parish, but in every other respect the church plays a full part in the diocese, including remitting a large quota to diocesan funds.

Another chapel which still survives is St John's, Downshire Hill, Hampstead. Built in 1823, 'and formerly the property of Lord Holland'. (See *A Short History of St John's, Downshire Hill, Hampstead*, available from its own church bookstall.) The new building became a proprietary chapel (private property), over which the vicar of Hampstead had practically no control. Also the new church had no parish assigned to it, and its minister's right of pastoral visitation was limited to those who joined the congregation'. (Notice the use of the word 'right'. Could such a concept really be defended in any relevant sense today?) The parish church of Christ Church, Brixton, was built on another proprietary chapel.

In Cheltenham St John's proprietary chapel was built in 1929 within the evangelical parish of Cheltenham, where the incumbent was Francis Close (later Dean of Carlisle). In later years it became a stronghold of 'tractarianism'. Although the worship at St John's Chapel was started in direct conflict with the incumbent's wishes, it continued for many years.

St Paul's, Portman Square, for many years a leading centre of evangelical witness and worship, was originally a proprietary chapel which eventually took on a parish structure, carved out of All Souls, Langham Place, to which it has now been returned.

Emmanuel Church, Wimbledon, itself a proprietary chapel, has started another congregation in a neighbouring parish where more than sixty people are worshipping in a school. The future of this is still under discussion with the bishop of the diocese of Southwark. Propriety chapels were numerous and special arrangements were by no means unusual.

The Oxford Movement

In the early days of the Oxford Movement small worshipping communities were formed in sympathetic establishments or homes in parishes where the local vicar was hostile or the local church was considered ineffective.

The Fellowship of the King

The Fellowship of the King with some 150 adult members is an interesting example of a free congregation in Bristol. Its founding pastor is the Rev. Stephen Abbott, formerly one of the university chaplains, who had charge of an inter-denominational chapel in the grounds of Wills Hall (one of the university halls of residence). After four years, Stephen planned to move into the parish ministry, on the understanding that he would be replaced as chaplain, but the diocese decided not to do so because of financial cut-backs. The congregation, which by this time (1980) included some graduates, undertook to support Stephen financially, and in January 1981 it was reborn as the Fellowship of the

King. There was a distinctly charismatic dimension to this community. Stephen was no longer licensed by the Bishop, but after a few months he was granted the Bishop's permission to officiate in the diocese. Initially, the main meeting for worship was in the evening, in the University Students' Union building, as the fellowship still consisted mainly of students. But in 1985, with fewer students and more Bristolians in the church, and influenced by the Ichthus Christian Fellowship in South London, Stephen began to plant small congregations in the areas of Bristol where members lived. This was done with the almost full agreement of the local clergy and pastors of all denominations. There are four such congregations, meeting mainly in school halls; the whole church still gathers as one large body for worship every Sunday night, now in the church hall of one of the local Anglican parishes. Stephen Abbott is in good standing with the diocese, and now has his permission to officiate renewed every three years. He also ministers happily as an Anglican priest in neighbouring parishes when requested, but he remains the leader of the team which runs this 'free' church. The whole enterprise is something that has evolved and the Bishop has had the wisdom to let it all happen whilst keeping careful watch. A more detailed account is to be found in Appendix C.

St Thomas, Crookes

An interesting experiment is currently taking place at St Thomas, Crookes in Sheffield, with the full knowledge of the Bishop, where the building is filled four times a Sunday. Its 9 o'clock Sunday night lay-led youthful congregation is engaged in reaching hundreds of other young people. It seems likely that they will soon have to move into a bigger building in someone else's parish! The Bishop recently confirmed ninety-eight from this late night congregation.

Nomination of deacons

We have a report of a situation still too sensitive at this stage to identify where a recent new incumbent is unsympathetic to the charismatic element he inherited from his predecessor. The bishop (a suffragan) has now authorised the lady deacon from that church to gather in her home the charismatics being lost to the church and has linked this group (through the deacon) to the vicar of a parish more in sympathy even though that parish is not an adjacent one to the home of the lady deacon.

An Anglican-Vineyard link

In one northern diocese there was an imaginative project under discussion whereby a medieval chantry chapel for which there was no longer any pastoral need might be made available to a Vineyard-type congregation. This is detailed in Appendix B.

Holy Trinity, Brompton

Holy Trinity Church, Brompton, has a number of pastoral groupings of some twenty to forty people made up of cells, each of which has five to eight members. The cells appoint their own leaders but the pastors of the groupings are appointed by the Holy Trinity, Brompton leadership and are responsible to a staff member appointed by the rector. These cells and groupings gather at locations well beyond the parish boundaries.

St Martin-in-the-Bullring, Birmingham, has study groups, etc., all over the city of Birmingham and even outside the diocese. St Andrew's, Chorleywood, has home groups extending out beyond the parish boundaries into three dioceses.

Baptismal policy

The Church of England permits lay hospital staff to baptise, irrespective of parish boundaries, where the patient is believed to be dying.

We hear reports, which we believe are well-founded, of a diocesan bishop who has advised his staff that where a local parish priest would not baptise a baby, or where the clergy from a given deanery had a policy supporting such a strict parish priest, then parents should shop around till they found a priest further afield who would baptise their child.

St Andrew's, Chorleywood

In our parish of St Andrew's, Chorleywood, two lay pastors from the neighbouring parish of Christ Church (our original mother church) are currently operating. A former assistant priest lived in our parish whilst working at Christ Church. Many other priests live outside their parishes (e.g. St George's, Leeds, St Mary's, Watford and for many years, not so long ago, there was one London vicar who lived in the Brighton area!).

Dispensations for mission

Partners in Mission reports on the Church of England have more than once recommended the establishment of 'mission areas', where existing ecclesiological legalities are suspended for a period.

Latin America

In South America we believe there are many Christian churches which do not even have a liturgy or a formally ordained leadership and which are linked together under an Anglican episcopal umbrella, for example, in the diocese of Northern Argentina, when it was under the leadership of Bishop David Leake, at that time the presiding bishop of the Southern Cone. This state will presumably have continued under the new bishop.

When 'La Igreja Episcopal', the Episcopal Church in Brazil was formed with its own bishops the English chaplaincies remained under the oversight of an English bishop from Buenos Aires, Argentina.

Europe

The same thing happened in Europe with the Bishop of Fulham overseeing some chaplaincy churches and an Episcopalian bishop from North America having overlapping oversight in the same area for other chaplaincy churches throughout Europe attached to military bases — e.g. Dusseldorf.

Scotland

A similar anomaly operated in Scotland in the cases of St Thomas' Church, Edinburgh and St Silas' Church, Glasgow — both under English diocesans for many years.

Individual exceptions

Canon Paul Oestreicher is licensed to operate within the Anglican Church, whilst retaining membership of the Society of Friends. He was even nominated for the office of a diocesan bishop in New Zealand whilst belonging to these two separate denominations!

A further local anomaly is the parish church of St Mary's, Rickmansworth, which has united with the Methodists. The Methodist minister is able to administer the sacrament of the Lord's Supper in this parish church and Anglican communicants participate. The scheme has the approval of the bishop. This kind of 'irregularity' is common practice in local ecumenical projects in many parts of the country.

Anglican clergy are still trustees for many missions – like Shaftesbury Crusade and London City Mission – which operate 'Free Churches' in existing parishes.

Salvation Army officers have traditionally maintained membership with their original churches, whilst opening halls where these ecumenical and gospel-loving Christians could evangelise.

Catholic practice

In South America the Roman Catholics cope with 'ineffective' parishes by allowing a religious order to start an alternative Catholic church which brings life into the area.

In the USA, where some of the Roman Catholic hierarchy appear to be hardening towards things charismatic within the traditional church setting, bishops have licensed charismatic communities to operate freely.

A similar kind of proposal in the UK comes from the *Cost of Conscience Movement* (which claims eleven episcopal supporters – not including retired bishops). An 'alternative episcopal oversight' whilst remaining within the Church of England is being seriously advocated by the movement as a 'fall back' position if the General Synod goes ahead with the ordination of women priests, according to a report in the *Church Times* (Nov 16, 1990).

We believe there is historical evidence to show that during the Black Death the Pope authorised members of the minor orders to celebrate mass with the dying.

The Lutheran Church

The Lutheran Church in Denmark has canons permitting the establishment of Elect Churches, of which there are some fifteen. These 'folkenkirken' choose their own pastor and support him financially. They also maintain his house and the church buildings. The official Danish Lutheran Church has no financial responsibility in such cases and the 'folkenkirken' are exempt from the State taxes which support the state church. Though the minister has been ordained and is licensed by the bishop, there is a great deal of freedom regarding liturgy and dress, provided the congregation are happy and agree to this. Elect Congregations may be allowed in some cases even to use the state church buildings without rent, when they are not otherwise in use. We quote a letter from a pastor of a 'folkenkirke' in Denmark (original spelling, expression and grammar):

As Elect Church we are members of the Danish Lutheran Church and is supposed to follow the rules and regulations of that church. In reality we have greater freedom as long as the Elect Church agree on doing things different because the tradition is that the bishop do not interfere.

So we follow liturgi in some areas, but we have worship instead of psalms; we have a team of preachers instead of only one person preaching, we encourage prophecy and use of spiritual gifts in the service; we have things for the children in the service and we try to have different people involved. About robes is the pastors supposed to be dressed as a pastor in the state church, i.e. he has the same possibilities for different dress up.

Organisation is formerly with the state church...

This recognition of the need for some kind of alternative structure has been in operation for over 100 years and followed a period of spiritual revival in Denmark, where otherwise the State church might have lost a large number of members.

ECUSA

It is interesting to read the *Church Times* headlines for 4 May, 1990: 'ECUSA Traditionalists Call For Own Province' and the 'Traditionalist' Episcopal Synod resolved last Friday to press for a tenth province of the Episcopal Church of the U.S.A. It would be a non-geographical province within the ECUSA, created for catholic and evangelical Episcopalians who are unalterably opposed to changes in their church's doctrine and discipline. The Synod believes that 'this proposal merits serious considerations within the Episcopal Church and the Anglican Communion generally. This plan presents the only realistic way for keeping together people of diametrically opposed theological outlooks. The Synod believes that 'some form of alternative episcopal oversight will have to be created. Merely ad hoc agreement between bishops is not an acceptable solution.' The situation is said to call for some definite institution of jurisdiction. But members of the Episcopal Synod of America (17,000 members) have reaffirmed their desire to remain within ECUSA.

These proposals have not been approved, but the very fact that they could be made by 'traditionalists' shows that 'structures' (parish, diocesan and provincial boundaries of a geographical nature) are secondary issues and not fundamental. The traditionalists give further examples of separate Anglican jurisdictions, e.g. the Maori Diocese of New Zealand and the Order of Ethiopia in Southern Africa, which are separate entities that are non-geographical and based on ethnic, cultural or linguistic lines. It was proposed that the 10th province would be a 'doctrinal' province. We quote this document to show how breaches of traditional concepts of church order are seriously proposed and considered where a situation would seem to demand it.

Peculiars

The organisaton of parishes into rural deaneries and deaneries into archdeaconries was not apparently complete until 1108. But claims for privilege were advanced from a conception of private ownership and allowances were made for 'peculiars' – churches which usually belonged to the lords on whose land they stood and whose ancestors had built them. Their incumbents in the eleventh and twelfth centuries were normally hereditary persons, married priests who passed on the churches to their sons, were a kind of vassal of their temporal lord, holding a benefice in return for service. Certain royal chapels and monastic congregations were also regarded as 'peculiars' (cf. Frank Barlow, *The English Church*, 1066–1154, Longman, London, 1979, pp 51–52).

Conclusion

Perhaps some of these random recollections have been chosen subjectively but we are sure there is enough substance to indicate precedents for variations or relaxations on ecclesiastical order, which, under certain circumstances, may be justified and temporarily tolerated.

Our later examples are taken from overseas, but they are worth noting, for there are other precedents which have already been effective in the change of Anglican structure, both within the Church of England and overseas, see for example, *The Case for Regional Episcopacy*, produced in Chile in 1968 and circulated at the Lambeth Conference of that year. Both the London and Sydney Dioceses (among others) seem to have taken this proposal seriously and subsequently introduced changes along the lines it advocated.

5

Dynamics in Church Growth

Throughout history there have been frequent outpourings of the Holy Spirit resulting in new life for the Church of God. These are too numerous to list here. A number of accessible books mention a fair selection, among which we would recommend *Enthusiasms* by Ronald Knox, SJ, Collins, London, 1987; *When the Spirit Comes with Power* by John White, Hodder & Stoughton, London, 1989, and *Power Evangelism* by John Wimber, Hodder & Stoughton, London, 1986.

All too often new movements of the Holy Spirit have been either syphoned off by an immature, ignorant or impatient local leadership or snuffed out by an intolerant establishment. Recently, and very encouragingly, this has not been so in every case as some recent examples will show.

Sheffield

A recent survey in Sheffield would appear to demonstrate that charismatic renewal amongst evangelical churches accounts for most of the church growth in that diocese. (See *Church of England Newspaper* January 26, 1990, p.9, Growth in the 90s by Bob Jackson).

Church planting

There are examples of charismatic churches today finding different ways of church planting – some within the structures, but others breaking through them. (See Grove Booklets on Evangelism Nos 4 and 8 *Church Planting: Models for Mission in the Church of England* by Bob Hopkins.)

1 In the eighties St Luke's, Cranham (Diocese of Chelmsford) under the Revd John Reeves, divided off into two new churches within the existing boundaries of his parish. (See Appendix F.)

2 Holy Trinity Church, Brompton, (Diocese of London) has burst out into three new churches – St. Barnabas, West Kensington, (separate deanery) St Marks, Battersea Rise (Diocese of Southwark – after 4 years of negotiation!) and St Paul's, Kensington.

3 Holy Trinity Church, Nailsea, (Diocese of Bath and Wells) has expanded into other new churches in the same parish – one began in a 'pub'.

4 St Andrew's, Chorleywood, (Diocese of St Albans) has planted two new fellowships within the parish, which meet on Sunday mornings. Arising out of a long programme for the training of lay folk there is the real prospect of further lay-led fellowships starting up in adjacent parishes. One has already begun in Watford.

5 St Mark's, Cheltenham, (Diocese of Gloucester) has a new off-shoot fellowship in another parish, currently led by the Revd Dr Nigel Scotland. This new congregation, 'The Glenfall Fellowship', started on January 7th, 1990, in the parish of St Mary, Charlton Kings. Dr

Scotland now has a licence for this for one year from the Bishop.

6   St Thomas, Crookes, (Diocese of Sheffield) have four different congregations (total 1,300–1,400 per Sunday) on the one site (total income around £300,000 per annum). The Nine O'Clock service at night is extremely radical, but very effective. This congregation has its own pastor – layman who has now been passed by ACCM. Another congregation of the same church is pastored by a Baptist minister.

A steady exodus from the Anglican church

There have been a great number of 'renewed' Anglicans leaving the Church of England over recent years. (Not all will necessarily be assets to the new communities they join!)

1   Some have formed or joined House Churches.

2   Some have been caught up with the London based Ichthus Fellowship, which is very active in church planting. In one instance, that Fellowship took over an almost empty building belonging to the Baptists, filled it and handed it back to the Baptists as a going concern.

3   Some have joined the new Vineyard Fellowships. At the moment these are all led by former Anglican priests, who are in no way rebels, but are prepared at some considerable sacrifice to step out in faith (they are not paid salaries from overseas) and plant new churches, where there can be more freedom and flexibility for containing the many laity who have no means

of exercising their gifts of leadership and ministry in the traditional churches. Like the Ichthus Fellowships mentioned above, they are also geared and motivated to reach out to the unchurched in the UK – those who have voted with their feet to ignore the traditional church.

4   Charismatic conferences in the UK are highly popular and probably far better attended than any other current religious gatherings. This is especially so of *Spring Harvest* and of John Wimber's conferences. The Rev. Colin Urquhart holds a large conference annually with several thousand attending, including a considerable number of Anglicans as do we ourselves at the Royal Bath and West Showground.

5   The Wimber conferences are for leaders and laity alike. About 35% of the leaders who attend are Church of England clergy. The latter return to their churches with a burden for renewal, which should naturally lead into church growth and then church planting. Where this is frustrated we risk losing a major dynamic for growth – something the church can ill afford to do.

6   The Rev. Charlie Cleverley (see his book *Church Planting* to be published by Scripture Union in 1991) relates the tragic case of Holy Trinity Church, Leicester, when the Revd John Aldis led that flourishing city centre church, which was outgrowing its accommodation. On two occasions, he applied to take over redundant or nearly redundant churches and on a third to start a new church. But in all cases it appears he was stopped by diocesan authorities as the centres were outside his parish. John Aldis has since moved to Hong Kong.

Thwarting new life

Can we afford to lose the blessing God is giving his Church by a blocking attitude of hostility, formal rejection, defensive pride or cold indifference towards the current Holy Spirit movements taking place in our churches today?

We recently suggested a man for a vacant living, where the Church had grown considerably over the last few years. The diocesan bishop (not St Albans, of course!), who was the patron, wanted assurances that the candidate we recommended would bring the two strands of the parish (renewed and traditional) together again. It is highly unlikely that any new vicar could carry out such a mandate successfully. The most probable result would be that, the younger renewed members would leave. However much we may deplore this, it is a reality which does not go away with episcopal pronouncements – too many people are voting with their feet. There must be a sensible realistic policy about this.

Whilst obviously committed to the unity of the Church, we must accept that the word of Christ: 'I did not come to bring peace, but a sword' (Mt. 10:34) is the painful, but inevitable reality in some situations.

Article 19 (of the Thirty-Nine Articles) is significant for any local church: *The visible church is a congregation of faithful men in which the pure word of God is preached and the sacraments duly administred according to Christ's ordinance.* Article 19 continues:

It is not necessary that Traditions and Ceremonies be in all places one or utterly like; for at all times they have been divers, and may be changed according to the diversities of countries, times and men's manners, so that nothing be ordained against God's Word.

But our own experience in church planting and our belief in the Holy Spirit convinces us that, given time, provided traditional bodies maintain a loving and respectful relationship, these new fellowships will discover for themselves the fuller riches of their inheritance from the traditional churches.

Providing the appropriate structure

Those clergy who are seeing new life in their parishes speak only too often of incredibly painful isolation from their dioceses if they identify openly with Renewal. Can the Church of England afford to go on aborting its new life in this way? Is there no way of harnessing this dynamic for new life? We believe there is. Our proposal is that the Church of England runs the old wineskins and new experimental ones in parallel – to have a double strategy, to borrow from Jürgen Moltmann. The new ones must be faithful to biblical doctrine, but may be flexible concerning traditional patterns of order, including parish boundaries, where it is appropriate.

Obviously the idea of any new wineskins becoming an expression of church growth beyond the traditional parish boundaries sounds disturbing and could appear to turn a great many of our parochial presuppositions on their heads.

It is important to note the following at this stage:

1   That pan-Anglicanism is not essentially built on parish boundaries. The Episcopal Church in the USA is not (though normally no new church building may be built within a limited distance from a currently functioning one). In South Africa most dioceses have parish boundaries, though this is not uniform (the Diocese of Port Elizabeth has no parish boundaries). In South America they have never had parishes. The Church of England need not be parochial.

2   The only real dynamic for church growth is the Holy Spirit. Those with experience in church growth and who have observed it closely in other denominations (we ourselves were involved in this for many years in South America) have found that 'strawberry-plant' growth aptly describes this natural process. This term was popularised by the Revd Dr Eddie Gibbs whilst working in our team in Chile and is meant to encapsulate the idea of a church naturally putting out runners, which become new plants. This is the normal way for some plants to grow.

The parish boundary, of course, inhibits such normal and natural growth because the whole country is already divided into parishes and the moment there are any feelers over the border then the appropriate ecclesiastical authorities will normally want to step in to shut it down.

3   As we have seen there are historical precedents for alternative and even overlapping ecclesiastical structures and the relaxation of traditional order.

6

The Way Ahead

Since there are recognised stages of congregational maturing, the time may come when the new wineskins will wish to become more integrated with other churches and desire a greater degree of order and acceptability. If they have been handled wisely there may be a request to the local bishop for a duly ordained leader. This will be the opportunity for the bishop to negotiate a greater degree of conformity, should it be felt to be still necessary at that stage.

We believe that though there may well be some pain (as with all birthing) the Holy Spirit seems surely to be leading the Church along this path. We do not claim it is the only way God will bring new life to the church, but, from our own experience both in South America and the UK, we are sure it is one way the Holy Spirit is urging us to move forward at this critical stage for our church today. It would be folly to snuff out such initiatives. It will bring glory to God if we start to see such new churches planted and the Kingdom of heaven extended.

We conclude with some words from the collective wisdom of the bishops of the Anglican Communion, expressed in their latest Lambeth Report (1988):

The pressing needs of today's world demand that there be

a massive shift to a mission orientatoin throughout the
Communion.

The mission and maintenance of the Church in the future
depend upon a radical commitment to the central role of the
laity.

The local congregation determines the agenda for the
Church at other levels, *whose principal vocation* is to respond
to and support the mission of the Church.

It costs the Anglican Communion many thousands of
pounds – much raised out of local church quotas – to
bring our bishops together. The price may seem very high
(as indeed it is), but will certainly not be begrudged if the
bishops are seen to be taking mission for new life seriously and appear to follow their courageous wisdom with
corresponding action. Life has to come before order! Our
structures must yield to mission. Mission is not to serve
the Church. The Church (never conceived by Christ as
something static) must serve the mission.

Appendices

Appendix A

St John's, Downshire Hill, Hampstead

St John's Downshire Hill, Hampstead, remains a Proprietary Chapel today but it is administered on similar lines to other Anglican churches. It has a church council, church wardens and other officers, but no official electoral roll. Not being a parish church, it is not licensed for weddings. These can only take place with an archbishop's licence. St John's is recognised as a church within the London diocese, but has a certain independence, mainly in financial matters. It receives no support from diocesan funds nor from the church commissioners and consequently it pays no diocesan quota. It is self-supporting in that the minister's stipend, repairs to the church and parsonage, and all incidental expenses are entirely borne by the congregation. However, St John's plays its part in the deanery and diocesan life and supports a number of missionary societies. St John's has remained conservative in its forms of worship and is noted for its strong sense of fellowship and freedom. It attracts others outside the Anglican fold with its definite evangelical witness.

Appendix B

The Church on the Bridge

In one northern diocese there was an imaginative project under discussion between John Wimber and the suffragan bishop.

John had been developing a favourite missiological theme. He pointed to the highly effective interplay between the *modality* and various *sodalities* which had been a prominent feature of the medieval church: between, that is to say, the main-stream church and a number of highly mobile and enterprising units of church life, mainly religious orders, who were given – or behaved as if they had been given – a degree of freedom from the strict rules imposed on everyone else by the Canon Law.

These adventurous Christians were thus enabled to be active in an effective way at the sharp end of the gospel, both abroad and in their home countries. Eventually the *sodality* was absorbed back into the *modality*, along with the spirituality which its freedom had enabled it to develop.

John Wimber had suggested that the Vineyard might have this kind of co-operative partnership with an Anglican diocese – though without the animosity which had frequently been part of the relationship three or four centuries ago.

The possibility under discussion had been the use by a Vineyard-type congregation of a medieval Chantry

Chapel, appropriately situated on a bridge, for which there was no longer any pastoral need in the parish where it was located.

The congregation's pastor would not have been under obedience to the Anglican bishop, or subject to Canon Law or to the ordinary rules of the Church of England. Nor, on the other hand, would he have had the benefit of the protection which that obedience provided. His relationship with the local clergy would have been confined to friendship and mutual prayer-support and fellowship in the Gospel.

The *sodality* would thus have been able to evangelise in its own way among people who were, in many instances, two generations away from even the folklore of the Christian religion.

After a few years in the Vineyard-type congregation many of the converts could well have found themselves at home in an Anglican setting which would have been bewildering to them had they ventured into it when they first came to faith. With trust on both sides there could have been two-way traffic between the two congregations, with fruitful consequences for both.

For various reasons – concerned with timing, and a plethora of local events requiring the concentrated attention of key local people, but not because of any hostility towards John Wimber and the Vineyard – this project did not get off the ground. John Wimber himself, though, had been sufficiently keen on what was being discussed to ensure that a substantial sum was put aside in the Vineyard budget to help fund the project in its initial stages.

Appendix C

The Fellowship of the King, Bristol

The Fellowship of the King, Bristol, developed out of a congregation of students from Bristol University who met for Sunday worship at the Monica Wills Memorial Chapel, a small building seating about 120 people set in the grounds of Wills Hall, one of the University halls of residence. This chapel had by statute to be interdenominational. When I arrived, it had a congregation of between eighty and one hundred worshipping students, which had been built up by my predecessor, Donald Werner (now vicar of St George the Martyr, Queen Square, London) from an original core of twelve. Donald could be characterised as evangelical, charismatic and well-qualified theologically. Under his clear teaching and uncompromising leadership, the chapel flourished, and became a popular centre of student Christian witness in the University.

The congregation consisted of a wide range of denominations: Anglicans, members of most Free Churches (including Pentecostal and House Church), and even a few adventurous Roman Catholics, together with those with no church background who had been converted through the ministry of the chapel. An Anglican chaplain was in charge simply because the Anglican chaplaincy, then with four chaplains, was the only one which could afford to release one full-time worker to the chapel.

There were two Sunday services. The morning one was relatively formal, and consisted of hymns, prayers, readings, an address and Holy Communion. The much freer evening meeting included the sharing of spiritual gifts, such as prophecies, tongues/interpretation, and healing. Every term there was a houseparty with a speaker, including well-known renewal leaders like Colin Urquhart and Michael Harper. But the further development and growth of the Fellowship owed a lot to the setting up of small mid-week groups for Bible-study, prayer and discussion. These cemented the community together, and inspired in some the commitment to stay in Bristol after graduation and be a church, no matter what the cost. Those students who did so became in effect the building blocks of the fellowship that was to emerge.

The catalyst for this unusual development was, simply, lack of money. In 1980, the Anglican Chaplaincy was told that, owing to financial cut-backs, it had to reduce its staff from four to three. At that time, I was intending to leave in any case in order to enter the parish ministry, thinking that I would be replaced by someone who could carry on the work of the chapel in a similar direction. However, this was not to be. It soon became clear that I was the chaplain who would not be replaced – leaving the chapel community without pastoral care or leadership. We all tried to think of ways of plugging this gap, but without success. It took six months for me to reach the inescapable conclusion that God wanted me to stay on, supported financially by the chapel community. I was initially most reluctant to take this step, as I did not want to be labelled a schismatic, and was indeed determined to work out my commitment to charismatic renewal within Anglicanism. However, God made it clear that I had to put the pastoral needs of the Fellowship before my own fears and prejudices. It was as if he painted me into a corner to make me walk through a door that I would otherwise have avoided like the plague.

When I wrote to the then Bishop of Bristol informing him of my plans, he was kind, but nonplussed. He could not formally license me to a non-Anglican job. After some months' reflection, however, he kindly gave me his permission (renewable annually) to officiate in Anglican churches in the diocese if invited to do so. The present Bishop has extended this permission over a renewable period of three years; on the two occasions I have seen him, he has shown great kindness and interest in what I am doing. So on 1st January, 1981, I became an Anglican priest working as a non-denominational Free Church pastor, supported financially by my own congregation, some of whom by that time had jobs in Bristol. I continued as a university chaplain, becoming, thanks to the support and approval of most of my chaplaincy colleagues of all denominations, the 'non-denominational' chaplain to the University. (I only laid down this ministry when the number of student members had dropped so much that the Fellowship no longer had a role as a chaplaincy church.)

We immediately renamed ourselves 'the Fellowship of the King', and moved our more informal evening meeting to the University Students' Union building, where it flourished. The morning meeting fell by the wayside, partly because we no longer had any reason to be formal, and partly because the Students' Union was closed on Sunday mornings. By this time, some of us had bought houses in the same area of Bristol, having decided that we would put a high priority on living close together and developing a sense of Christian community. After consultation and prayer, we had felt led to south Bristol, and had finally chosen Knowle, where one graduate was already working. Most of the other Fellowship members

lived either in Clifton, near the University, or in the
Stoke Bishop halls of residence.

For the first four years of the Fellowship's existence,
the only morning meetings were prayer meetings taking
place in a house in Knowle and a student's room in Stoke
Bishop. However, in 1984 we felt it right to start church-
planting by establishing a worshipping congregation in
Clifton (where most of our members were then living). In
this we had been influenced by Ichthus Christian Fellowship of South London. My pastoral assistant had taken
part in their August church-planting project, and I had
met and talked extensively with their leader, Roger Fors-
ter, while he was leading a university mission in Bristol
in 1983. I was (and still am) convinced that church-planting is the best means of church growth, provided that
there are enough committed people to do it.

For me as an Anglican minister, this has meant the
alien process of planting a congregation in another Anglican minister's parish. I found this idea positively offen-
sive at first, so conditioned was I by traditional Anglican
respect for the parish boundary. But as there seemed no
way round the problem, I tried to tackle it in the most
open and loving way possible. Once we had found a place
to meet (a small local hall), we wrote to all the local
ministers informing them of our existence as four home-
groups in the area, and letting them know of our plans to
start a Sunday morning service. In the same letter, I
applied for the Fellowship to join the local Council of
Churches, and for me and my assistant to join the Ministers' Fraternal. The application was accepted, and my
assistant soon found himself the Secretary of the Council.
Only two of the fifteen or so ministers had any problem
with what we did. Both were Anglican, and one of them
did not in any case himself have anything to do with the
Ministers' Fraternal.

Since then, we have planted three other congregations

(in Knowle, Southville and Bishopston), which we call 'community churches', and have joined three other Councils of Churches. I have only experienced any difficulty with one other Anglican minister (who questioned our right to exist in his parish), but this was not a serious problem. The Bishop has had no occasion to reprimand me or ask that I stop doing what I am doing. I have found some of my colleagues to be initially suspicious, and when I first attend a Ministers' Fraternal I am occasionally treated to searching questions and hostile comments. For example, I was once accused of being a 'Gnostic', out of touch with the real world – presumably, living on some sort of charismatic 'high'. Ironically, this was at a time of deep problems in relationship within our church, when I was having to sort out some very difficult and down-to-earth situations. However, after this initial rough ride, I have found that I am accepted as a normal human being, and made very welcome. In particular, I have found my local Fraternal in Knowle to be very supportive, and was delighted to be able to serve for a year as Chairman of our local Council of Churches.

Our philosophy of church-planting has been, first, that we should be as careful as possible not to alienate other church leaders and Christians in the area by acting independently – hence the desire to join the local Council of Churches, and to be involved in inter-church activities as much as possible. Second, we do not wish to steal other people's sheep; our goal is church growth by conversion, not by transplantation. Third, we do not wish to be superior in our thought, speech or behaviour, giving the impression that we are better Christians or more spiritual than the other churches. We have to be very honest with ourselves and with God about this, because it is a real temptation. Fourth, we view the area where we live as vitally important, as it is the place where our evangelism and interaction with the community actually occur. Fifth, we regard the evangelisation of our nation, and specifically of Bristol, as of prime importance. As only an average of 10% of the population have any commitment to a local church, it seems to us that any committed Christians have a mandate for church-planting. One practical example of our outreach into the community is *Kingfisher*, a mums and toddlers group in Knowle. Started initially by one of the mums, an experienced nursery teacher, in a small hall that was draughty and far from ideal, the group flourished and eventually moved to the much larger and more suitable modern hall of the local Methodist church, with the approval of the minister. Through this group, contact has been made with a number of non-Christians, and at least three people have so far become Christians and joined the church as a result.

We have a basic commitment to the threefold expression of our Fellowship as 'cell/congregation/celebration'. The *cell* is represented by the Home Group (consisting of at least ten members), the *congregation* by the local 'community church' (our morning meetings), and the *celebration* by the larger gathering on Sunday evening when the community churches come together. There are difficulties in holding together the local involvement with the commitment to the wider church family, but we remain convinced that local church-planting is the way forward for church growth. I am profoundly grateful to God and the Bishop of Bristol for making it possible for me to lead our developing Fellowship without having to break with my Anglican roots, and I am delighted to have been so warmly accepted by existing local churches, and to be able to work in harmony with them.

Stephen Abbott, 28.12.90

Appendix D

Local Community Churches in Chester-le-Street

When he was Bishop in Chile, I remember David Pytches describing church growth in South America. He said it was like the strawberry plant. The parent churches sent out 'runners'. These were small off shoots, little congregations established at a distance from the originating church. In time, like strawberry runners, they would establish and root themselves in the new setting to provide a new Christian church in the neighbourhood. In this way, the churches in Latin America were multiplying by dividing. I thought, when I heard about it, that this was a good picture to describe the way the church was growing, and the congregations multiplying, in our town in the North East of England. Although it was a totally different context, the same thing was happening in Chester-le-Street as was happening in Chile. Although the story which follows covers the last twenty years, to understand what has been happening we have to go back long before 1971.

Chester-le-Street is a town of some 30,000 people in the North East of England, lying about half way between the cathedral city of Durham and the industrial city of Newcastle. The town enjoyed its hey-day 1,100 years ago when it was the centre of pilgrimage. Kings, bishops and humble folk would travel from all over the nation to visit the shrine of the North East's favourite saint, Cuthbert. It must have been something like having a first division football club in the town. People came from all around in an expectant mood, and the little community grew and flourished.

The Vikings, with their reputation for murder, pillage and rape, changed all that. It was their threat that originally brought the little community of St Cuthbert to the town with their precious relics in *AD* 883. Under the threat of further Viking invasions, 112 years later, the monks moved on from the town to settle eventually in Durham. Thereafter, Chester-le-Street entered upon the ups and downs of a fairly typical parish, with the church very much at the centre of village life.

When they began to sink new coal mines in the nineteenth century, the population began to multiply and the churches, with the Methodists at the forefront, began to plant new churches in the little outlying mining communities. The famous bishop of Durham, Hensley Henson, used to complain that, when he visited the pit villages, the foundation stones of the Methodist chapels always seemed to record a date earlier than the founding of any Anglican mission church.

In the years following the Second World War, the pits began to close and the mining villages went into decline. Unlike some parts of the North East, however, Chester-le-Street made a successful transition: it became a dormitory town. Being at the centre of a network of good roads, it has retained its popularity as a convenient place to live, even though it has shared the same depressing symptoms of high unemployment and slow decay of the industrial North East. In short, the population continued to increase, and the trend continues today.

The town now consists of a number of different estates, linked by roads which radiate from the town centre. They form a cluster of what one might call urban villages, retaining many of their historical links with local mining communities. These have been supplemented by new housing developments, often inhabited by the children of the older residents. The town, therefore, is a fairly homogeneous unit which comprises a number of smaller similarly homogeneous estates and villages. In other words, Chester-le-Street is a fairly popular self-contained community with many people coming from similar backgrounds and sharing the same interests.

The town is made up of one Anglican parish. There are also Methodist, Roman Catholic, Salvation Army, United Reformed and Pentecostalist congregations. The churches, with the exception of the Anglicans, have lately concentrated their work in the middle of the town. It is important to understand at least a little of the background if one is to have any appreciation of the developments in the life of the Anglican church over the last twenty years, and to understand why it has grown and the congregations have multiplied. As the population grew, new estates sprang up, at a distance from the parish church. There was no visible Christian corporate presence or witness within them. Few of the residents had more than occasional links with the parish church, and those were through baptisms, weddings and funerals. It became imperative to take the church to the people, a strategy the Methodists had pioneered more than a hundred years before.

The Anglican congregation began to reach out as it had done, after the Methodist example, when it established mission churches, often cheaply built, in the mining villages. This time, however, the twentieth century strategy was somewhat different. They established area congregations, or 'family services' as they were called, where the people lived. In Africa they would probably have been called out-stations. In South America, some of them might even have been described as Base Communities. The Archbishop of York, when he was Bishop of Durham, called them dispersed congregations. Others have described them as satellites. If one wanted to be technical, one could call them semi-autonomous congregations, but more of that below. In Chester-le-Street they followed the model of the strawberry plant, with the 'runners', small groups of Christians resident in a neighbourhood, establishing new 'plants', area congregations or community churches, which rooted themselves at a distance from the 'parent', parish church, before establishing a semi-autonomous life of their own.

OUTLINE MAP OF CHESTER-LE-STREET

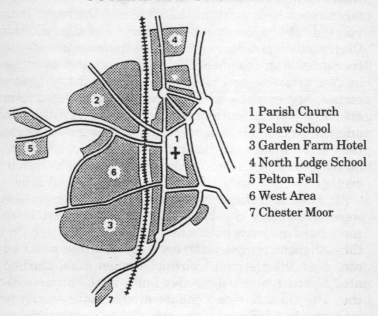

1 Parish Church
2 Pelaw School
3 Garden Farm Hotel
4 North Lodge School
5 Pelton Fell
6 West Area
7 Chester Moor

The congregations started in different ways. One developed and grew from a Sunday School which used to meet in a church day school building. One, in an ex-mining community, moved when the old mission church literally collapsed. But it started again in a new form in the village hall, at a new time and in a new style designed to draw in a different and younger group of worshippers. Patrick Blair, who was the originator of this strategy in the town in 1971, then identified a huge estate which had no centre for Christian worship or, indeed, any centre for public meeting other than the neighbourhood pub. Some of the congregation of the parish church who lived on the estate began a service there which grew and grew until it eventually had to move into the local comprehensive school. We were now committed to opening area services in all the centres of population in our town. At times, it was a slow painstaking business. Isabel Wells visited faithfully in one of the council housing estates for many years before commencing services in the Residents' Social Club at the festivals, and then successfully multiplied them until they became a weekly gathering of the faithful in that part of the parish. We ended up with seven local community services, in addition to the more traditional acts of worship which continued in the beautiful and ancient parish church in the centre of the town. Incidentally, the numbers attending there were surprisingly and quickly recouped after the opening of each new worship centre.

At first, of course, the new dispersed congregations were heavily dependent upon the parish church for the resources necessary to sustain their life. In the early days they even had to make use of tape-recorded sermons and music. Ordinands from nearby Cranmer Hall, Durham, also played a significantly leading role. Over the years they enjoyed an increasing autonomy until, now, they are largely responsible, with the clergy for their own life and activities, whilst retaining an ongoing link with the wider congregation through regular united services and participation in the parochial church council. The fuller story, with its ups and downs, has been told elsewhere. (Ed. Eddie Gibbs, *Ten Growing Churches*, MARC Europe, Bromley, 1984, pp 126–143. Ian Bunting and Jim Brewster, *1883–1983 The Eleventh Century of the Parish Church in Chester-le-Street*, Parish Office, Chester-le-Street, 1984, pp 51–67. Ian Bunting, 'Focus on Models of Ministry – Following the Strawberry Plant', *Partners*, No 10, Summer 1985, pp 3, 4.) There are, however, some important connections with the developments which have been taking place, at the same time, in other parts of the world. We are talking about the working out of important aspects of Christian mission.

The pioneers of the area congregations, community churches, in Chester-le-Street had a three-fold purpose:

1 The local community church would provide a Christian *presence* in the communities where the people lived. In each of the estates in the town the schools, halls, clubs, and even a pub, provided possible venues for community activities. They enabled the local Christians to come together for Sunday worship in a meeting place big enough to accommodate local families and to provide ancillary rooms for Christian education. Some of these places were not without their hazards. It is not ideal to preach across the pool table, with the go-go dancers' cage as a backdrop. How far did people judge us guilty, by association, when the morning service in the Social Club was followed by the Sunday midday striptease performance? It was not long, however, before local residents recognised these unlikely venues as centres of worship, no matter what else also took place there. They became places where people turned to Christ, where the children learned the Christian truths, where parents brought their children for baptism, and, latterly, where the faithful gather to celebrate the Supper of our Lord. One day a child saw the brewer's dray delivering beer to the pub where the family worshipped on Sundays. He asked his

parents, 'Why are they delivering beer to our church?' He had got the message. The pub had become a sign of the Christian presence we were trying to provide at the heart of the community.

2 The local community church would take pastoral *responsibility* for the area in which the congregation met. This represented a clear devolution of responsibility from the parish church to the area congregation. The local Christians took responsibility for pastoral emergencies of one sort or another as well as the pastoral care of families in connection with baptism, marriage and funerals. Nearly all of them attempted some kind of evangelistic outreach in the neighbourhood through 'Getting-to-know-you' evenings or Basic Christianity groups. Each of the local community churches exercised a responsibility for the wider community in a different way. One started a play group, welcomed Vietnamese Boat People, campaigned for a BMX track and tried to get a housing project for the single homeless off the ground. Another began an aerobics club. Another was closely involved in the local residents' association. Another ran a community youth club and promoted social events in the local school. The area congregation, which met in the parish church, was largely instrumental in pioneering an effective domiciliary care service for the terminally ill which became a recognised service throughout the town. We worked in harmony with the well tried policy of Dr Schuler (Santa Ana, California), 'Find a need and meet it. Find a hurt and heal it.'

3 The local community church would offer a *witness* to the Gospel. Apart from evangelistic efforts, often associated with itinerant evangelists and the major Christian and Folk festivals, like Mothers' Day and Harvest Thanksgiving, the Christians witnessed mainly through well-tried evangelistic methods and, possibly more effectively, through small task-orientated groups.

For example, we ran an 'Agnostics Anonymous' group. At the time, it seemed exceedingly fruitless. One man, however, after a journey that took him all of eight years, did eventually come to a living faith in Christ. Others came to faith through pub nights for men, with a challenging testimony or talk to spark off an animated interchange that usually lasted all evening. At times, it seemed we were promoting an endless series of coffee mornings and supper evenings. I came to understand the evangelist who once said that, if he were given £1,000 he would spend it on food. We were trying, in the context of warm locally-appropriate Christian hospitality, to take the opportunity to bear effective witness to a living gospel. It worked. This kind of outreach added members to the worshipping congregation.

The establishing of area, or family, services was the means chosen to achieve the mission of those who started the local community churches in Chester-le-Street. In other words, they would evangelise by giving the parish church an evangelistic structure. It was a structure for evangelism rather than a method. The methods, and many different methods of evangelism were used, served the structure. Geoffrey Walker, the present rector of the parish, summed it up when he wrote, 'We are building an indigenous church in focussed communities. The goal is evangelisation.'

Ian Bunting

Appendix E

Mobile 'Seed' Teams
and Cross Cultural Planting

My wife Mary and I were both born and brought up in the Chorleywood/Rickmansworth area which is commuterland to the North-West of London. We both attended our local parish churches (Christ Church, Chorleywood and St Mary's, Rickmansworth, respectively) in our childhood and through to our early teens. We both then fell away from any regular church involvement after leaving school.

It was not until 1973 when we had both passed thirty that we each found a living faith in Jesus and began to experience healing of a broken marriage. Soon afterwards the Lord gave us an increasing conviction of the UK as a mission field needing missionary strategies. This sense came through visits to churches, Bible reading and seeing the empty eyes and hopeless faces thronging the city streets. We also received mental impressions or 'pictures' of the nation as a grey barren spiritual desert.

Through a combination of hearing from missionaries on furlough and our own developing ideas, we sensed that God's mission strategy for the UK would involve a key role for church planting. In fact by the end of 1974 we had a clear vision for church planting and a strong personal call that this was the ministry that we were to give our lives to.

At the heart of this church planting vision was a passion that teams were crucial to this mission model. The strength of a team would be that it would be the embryo church from day one. Secondly, relationships between team members would be the resource to enable pioneering of hard areas and thirdly, the range of gifts of the different team members would be the dynamic resource for rapid growth and development of the emerging new church.

Our desire to see every member of a team (and of a whole local church for that matter) develop their own ministry to the full, made me negative towards the concept of ordination as I saw it in the traditional pattern of denominational church one man leadership. I was therefore very resistant when I felt that God might be asking me to submit to Anglican theological training and ordination. However, the message seemed to be that if you wanted to share ministry with others – someone first had to have the church's authority before he could give it away! I hoped that I had got it wrong and quite expected to be turned down at each step in the selection process – I was very direct and open when sharing our call with the Diocesan Director of Ordinands, the bishop, college panel and ACCM selectors. To each in turn I related our story of a church planting vision for the UK and of a calling to teams and of giving the ministry away. To our great surprise this only produced smiles, nods and acceptance for training and ordination.

We were led to take up non-stipendary ministry. This was not in order to follow the usual model of enabling spare time ministry/ministry at the workplace – but, rather, was because self-supporting 'tent making' ministry seemed to us the most common biblical pattern for church planters. We could also see that most areas requiring a pioneer team would by definition be unable to offer financial support and hence the combining of a flexible paid job with ordained ministry was likely to be ideal.

God also played his 'trump card' in this development. When our vicar thought he had arranged for us to see someone to pursue stipendary ordination training at Oakhill Theological College, we found to our surprise that the man who interviewed us was in fact the director of a new experimental scheme of ministry training just starting in the St Albans diocese that we had never heard of! Having 'cast his line', God 'baited the hook' with the fact that this new programme sought to recognise much wider ministries than before. In fact they were open to license people to ministries there had been no names for previously. This not only coincided with our concept of multiple ministries – but also enabled Mary to train with me for the three years and then to be licensed for counselling and healing work.

We were able to stay in Christ Church, Chorleywood during this 'sandwich course' type of training and on its completion in 1979 we joined the staff under the vicar, Peter Sertin. Even though we could see no direct opportunity for any church planting type of ministry, I changed my job to enable a four-day week salaried employment with an accountancy firm. This at least began to prepare us by starting the adjustment to combine two jobs and a lower income level.

As we waited for the door to open to church planting two significant developments occurred. Firstly, through my parents' involvement with Barry Kissell's faith-sharing teams at St Andrews, Chorleywood, the opportunity came for Mary and I to take part in some of those team visits to churches. Then Barry asked us if we would lead a team of our own, largely of members from Christ Church. This gave us invaluable experience. We not only had the chance to visit many different churches up and down the country but we also learnt key lessons in working and ministering together in a team. The exciting opportunities to share life and renewal with church members over a weekend or to help work with them over a week in evangelism and outreach was satisfying on one level but also seemed to further stimulate our underlying calling to church planting. Return faithsharing visits to the same parish after a year made us aware how much more could be achieved by 'residential faith-sharing' – a team ready to permanently relocate. We could see that such a resource was likely to transform the ability of a weaker church to embrace and work through the new life and ministry of which the short-term teams gave a glimpse.

The second significant development arose out of the counsel of a friend with whom we shared our frustration at not being able to see any way forward for real church planting initiatives for us in the Church of England. On his suggestion we spoke to the leaders of the two Anglican churches in Chorleywood. With their agreement, we then approached the people with whom God had already given us a relationship and whom we sensed might share and understand our church planting vision and who potentially could be future team members. We started to meet together periodically (about every 6 weeks on average) with the purpose of praying together and asking God to speak and develop the vision. Out of this a group of about fifteen was formed. These were a great encouragement to us and our experience of God together did continue to sharpen the vision.

During this period of waiting, two possible opportunities to plant new churches arose but neither actually materialised. The first was when our vicar, Peter Sertin, questioned whether there might be a future in planting within the Christ Church parish. He mentioned either a private housing estate or a council estate as possibilities (a plant has eventually begun on the latter in September

1990 with a family service held in a local junior school).

The second door which seemed to open, at least a crack, was in 1981 in the neighbouring parish across the diocesan boundary. This was a combined parish including St Michael's in the tiny village of Chenies (about 150 inhabitants) and St Georges in the large community of Little Chalfont (with some ten thousand residents). Both churches had very small congregations and following closure of the evening service at St Georges, a teenage/ young twenties youth group had been allowed to start their own Sunday evening youth service with the help and encouragement of half a dozen youngsters from the church youth group that we helped to lead. This led to meetings that I had with the vicar and one of the wardens. The warden was very keen that this initiative grow into something of a church plant with us heading up a team to build on the new beginnings of the evening service and to mobilise relevant outreach into the hundreds of flats and estate houses around the church. In time, he envisaged that this might involve growth and change in the morning service – already the evening youth team helped lead this once a month and I had been asked over to help lead both services and build relationships.

This door finally shut after some six months of the developing relationship when, at the vicar's request, the diocese of Oxford appointed a curate to the parish. The door which did eventually stay fully open was neither within the parish nor in a neighbouring area. It came as something of a Macedonian call – 'Come over to Parr Mount and help us.' Parr Mount is at the opposite quarter of the country in the North West of England. This opening came through a contact made during a faith sharing visit.

In 1981 and 1982 we were members of teams led by Barry Kissell to St Mark's, Haydock in St Helen's, Merseyside. The second visit for ten days saw an amaz-

ingly fruitful time of outreach with scores of folk coming
to new faith in Christ. Barry was so moved by the mission
that he spent the following week in prayer and fasting
asking God whether there was special significance in this
near-revival experience. On the Saturday, a phone call
came from Chris Woods, the vicar of Parr Mount, another
parish in St Helens who had already requested a visit.
This long telephone conversation led Barry to believe
that St Helen's was the place we should move to! He
immediately phoned us that day and recommended we
contact Chris Woods, arrange a visit, get our team
together, sell our house and move up to Holy Trinity
parish!

This parish was very different from St Mark's,
Haydock. The area was an urban industrial UPA made
up of very depressed council estates and some old ter-
raced housing. The church was equally depressed with
only some 30–40 members, just a handful of whom lived
within the parish. At that time in early 1982, Chris
Woods had been vicar for some two and a half years most
of which had been totally discouraging. There were just
the faint signs of the beginning of new life and Chris in
conversation with Barry was most keen to explore the
possibility of a team coming to help him with the re-
planting of an effective local congregation to bring Christ
to that desperate situation.

Our first two visits confirmed that it was the last place
to which we would choose to move! However, our hearts
were immediately knit together with Chris and his wife
Kathy and we were encouraged by seeing God use us in a
small but significant way with one of the local people who
'happened' to call at the vicarage on the first day we were
there. It was also good to hear from Chris that the tide
had begun to turn in the church. In his first two years,
despite all the prayer they had put in, things only got
worse. However, since November '81 there had been signs

of hope with a slow but steady trickle of local people becoming converted. These developments were to be the foundations of the planting of a new UPA congregation.

For us back in Chorleywood, there began the testing of a team calling to St Helens. It was not nearly such a quick process as Barry's first phone call had suggested. Our group continued to meet and we now regularly exchanged insights received with Chris Woods. These all tended to confirm that we were now looking at the right opening and things were getting exciting.

Knowing that Barry had been invited by Chris Woods to take a faith sharing team to Parr Mount in November '82, I asked Barry to include in the team some of those who had been most positive about a move with us. We trusted that the weekend mission would give a good chance to test their calling to Merseyside. The weekend came just after John Wimber's first visit to St Andrews and the team saw some amazing and wonderful things begin to happen amongst the small core group at Parr Mount. It certainly seemed that God was initiating something special there.

However, in the months that followed, one after another of the group members/couples told us that they did not feel it right to move to St Helens. This was principally a case of not sensing God's confirmation – although in a couple of cases there were complications of serious illness of ageing parents, the expected arrival of a first child and a house move. All these things emphasised to us the difficulty and the cost of being part of a mobile church planting team.

They also left Mary and I with an acute dilemma. As those in the group who had seemed most likely to accompany us decided it was not right for them, other means of guidance continued to give green lights for a move to St Helens. One of the other main tests of this calling was with those in authority over us. By now David Saville was

vicar at Christ Church, Chorleywood, and as we shared
with him at each step he moved from being cautiously
positive to eventually believing that it was certainly right
for us to make the move.

The bishops at each end were also consulted. Whereas
Dr Runcie had first known of our general vision, it was
now to Bishop John Taylor that we went in our own diocese of St Albans. He asked most searching questions
which helped us to see more clearly the key issues in such
an unconventional move. He saw that the nearest parallel to our model of mission was the case of a small community of an order (such as the Franciscans) establishing
themselves as a resource within a parish. He wisely
warned of the danger of us being seen as a permanent
'outsider group' and was relieved to know that all in our
team would see themselves as fully an organic part of the
local congregation and in any later move, a new team
would arise which could be composed of some of the original 'in comers' with other local Christians. At the end of
our time together Bishop John felt it right to recommend
that we go – being assured of a welcome back if our step of
faith in fact proved not to work out in the event. His final
prayer for us we felt had real prophetic force and
strengthened us greatly.

Our visit to Bishop David Shepperd in Liverpool was
very different but also finished on a very positive note. He
had first requested that we see John Roberts, the chairman of the Diocesan Evangelism Committee to 'screen'
the whole idea. Then we saw Bishop David in '82/3 with
Chris Woods. The interview had a difficult start in which
we explored such institutional matters as the possible
effect of our move on Sheffield quotas, whether Mary's
licence in St Albans would be transferable and clarified
that neither of us would be expecting any stipend. Then
suddenly the Bishop asked us what was 'our dream'.
From this point things became much more positive. As we

shared, Bishop David asked us what answers we thought we brought to the urban mission challenges of Parr Mount. Our reply was 'none' – 'only a conviction that on our own we couldn't hope to achieve anything, we would need to learn when in the situation, trust the Holy Spirit's guiding and equipping and also expect that we would be more effective in encouraging and building up local Christians who would relate much better in evangelism to their own neighbours and friends'. This seemed to reassure the Bishop who understandably would not want a team of 'slick' outsiders thinking they had all the answers.

Following this visit the way was open for us to move. However, our whole concept was of a team – and where were our fellow members! We went through several agonising months of deep confusion as we tried to reconcile the clear call to 'Go' with the absence of the team that was the foundation of our calling. In the end God clearly spoke to me – saying that I had to leave the team to Him. We were to fast and pray, proceed to move and trust Him for the rest.

So in July 1983 Mary and I finally moved to a two up/ two down terrace in Parr Mount – some fifteen months after Barry's momentous phone call! At that point none of our group from Chorleywood accompanied us – but God had begun to build his team! He had quite independently given the idea to Kathy Woods one Sunday morning as she played the piano that they invite John and Michele Walker to join them from YWAM in Sussex. They in fact moved into the parish with the family six weeks before us. Then three months after our move, Tim Humphreys from St Andrews, Chorleywood, who was a member of our group, finally decided he wanted to come and join us. So, the team of seven including the Woods, was formed.

Our early experiences were good although they confirmed that church planting in practice is not glamorous.

We experienced the pains of a team being welded together from four different churches. We felt the personal limitations of cross-cultural church planting as we had to let go of so much of our middle class background. Church planters always should aim to give away their ministry to others, but with our ignorance of culturally appropriate models for this northern UPA parish we had constantly to hold back and let patterns emerge from local people. In this respect, our experience has confirmed the suitability of a smallish 'seed team' for mobile, cross-cultural plants. We can see the potential dangers of setting up a 'rejection syndrome' if there is too sizable a 'transplant'.

On the other hand, we did use to the full short-term visits of mission teams to boost resources for local mission and evangelism. Another key was Barry Kissell's visit for ten days with a team in November '83 when we saw dozens of locals respond to Jesus in informal home discussion groups. The town-wide mission with Eric Delve in March '84 followed by Billy Graham at Anfield in August, produced so many local responses that from then on the task was discipleship and establishment in church, tasks that we were to discover would take on average two years with people who came from such broken and depressed backgrounds.

Nonetheless, within two and a half years of moving we could say that the planting process begun by Chris and Kathy on their own, had been successfully completed, with well over a hundred in the church. The team had played a key part in this. How vital to the faithfulness was the common vision and philosophy of ministry which had formed the foundation of our relationship with the Woods and Tim Humphrey. There were many trials, tears and frustrations alongside experiencing the power of God in many new ways. Events led the church to near bankruptcy, to moving into a hall and a hired school – but through it all was a steady growth as many found the grace of God bringing light, life and hope to their desperate circumstances.

It was by no means all success, ground was gained at a high price and we can look back on mistakes and many still unanswered questions. But after three years, first one and then two others of the team moved on into new ministries. Significantly they were not the only ones 'sent' out from this newly planted church. We believe that the principle is that...each multiplies 'according to its own kind'. It is not surprising therefore that this church, planted with the help of a mobile missionary team model, has seen eight members sent out and supported in full time church ministry and missionary service.

Robert Gardner-Hopkins

Appendix F

Limits to Growth Within the Parish

Eight years ago we began work in Cranham, a suburb of Upminster on the edge of Greater London. People had been coming to Christ and the church was growing. We soon found that, though the surroundings were drab, the people were alive with love for God. In addition to the usual duties of a curate, I worked as leader of a faith sharing team, which was sent out to many parishes, leading weekends of renewal and weeks of mission. Soon after I arrived, with the parish church St Luke's nearly full (it seats about 250), one of the curates took a team of twelve adults from the church to form a new congregation in a disused Brethren Hall given to us free of charge. St Luke's spent £40,000 on the building, gave away one of its full time staff and several of its members and the new church began to grow slowly but surely.

Then just over two years later, John Reeves, the vicar, announced at the AGM (an opportunity we use to set spiritual and practical goals for the year to come) that as St Luke's was full again, he felt the time had come for church number three. He asked those interested or intrigued by the idea to pray about whether God might be calling them personally to this work. Testing a call to such work is important. Suffice it to say that within a few months, we gave up travelling and took a team of sixteen adults plus their children out of St Luke's and began Cranham Community Church. Here we had the opportunity to hire a secular building. In 1987 we were given a permanent office in the community centre and hired its hall on Sundays: all for only £2,000 a year. After a struggle this grew to a membership of around a hundred within three years.

During these months, we found that we were part of what amounts to a movement in Britain today with churches springing up everywhere.

The numbers mentioned above are very small, but not if they are multiplied hundreds and hundreds of times across the nation. In the last years, it has become clear that many other churches are working in this way in every denomination. My view is that this is the work of the Holy Spirit, planting hundreds of small, vital congregations in schools, pubs, gymns, wherever a hall can be hired. David Pawson once said: 'My ambition is to find out what God is doing and join in.' It has been a privilege to 'join in' in a very small way with what God is doing in the country.

About four years after we planted our first congregation, the parish gathered everyone together for a morning service. We hired a local school and the congregation numbered over 400. Thus we saw that our morning congregation had doubled in size through this strategy.

There are many biblical and pragmatic reasons for church planting which I deal with at length in my book, *Church Planting: Our Future Hope*, published by Scripture Union. Briefly, such a strategy expresses love for the lost; breaks through prejudice (with the mother church); breaks with offputting traditions; brings faster growth; promotes personal growth among those who take part; takes more ground for the Kingdom of God. In church growth terms, another pressing reason is that it is a way of expanding a full church. Peter Wagner has said: 'Strangulation...occurs when the physical facilities can no longer accommodate the people flow. Sanctuary seating space is one of the vulnerable areas for strangulation. If in any regular service over 80 per cent of the seats are taken, the church is already losing potential members.' Many 'thriving' churches need to take heed of this and see that growing can be a better sign of life than to have more or less filled the same building for twenty years. To grow may well mean for some to move house and there can be many tensions associated with this upheaval. But it is worth it if the number of those being made disciples increases significantly.

In the process of expansion, we have found the model in Acts 13:2 and 3 helpful: 'While they were worshipping the Lord and fasting, the Holy Spirit said, "Set apart for me Paul and Barnabas for the work to which I have called them." So after they had fasted and prayed, they placed their hands on them and sent them off.' We see here Paul had first heard the clear call; then been given a clear commission from the others at Antioch; he then pursued a clear course of action before seeing clear conversions and churches planted. Once we have this vision to start a new congregation, our experience has been to seek a leader first of all. He needs to be called by God and then his team (anything from a dozen to a hundred) needs similarly a clear call. This needs to be expressed to and tested by the church leadership. Then a clear commissioning and public sending out with the laying on of hands is healthy. This helps the sending church to see why members of the Church Planting Team are laying down all their other responsibilities. Thirdly, the clear course of action is then worked out, preferably in writing, in terms of a five year plan. This calls for patience and hearing from God as the programmes to match the vision are drawn up. Finally, the team will be looking for clear conversions: people who are added to the new church and who grow up within it to lead others in their turn.

In 1989, with John Reeves having moved to the Midlands, the bishop and wardens took the unusual step of inviting me to become the next vicar: thus continuity of vision was secured. Among other things I did in my first year was informally to change our umbrella name to Cranham Park Fellowship (C. of E.) This is just one minor example of how we have stated clearly that the Parish Church is but one part of our church, with Moor Lane, Community Church and now Park Estate Churches as equally important.

We have not aimed at making these congregations independent, partly because of the small distances between them. Our structure is to ask everyone to meet midweek in a housegroup relating to the congregation they attend. The congregations then meet separately on Sunday morning for family worship. We then encourage all who can to come together for a joint celebration on Sunday night.

We sent out our third church planting team about six months ago, targeting a council estate. By contrast to Ichthus Christian Fellowship in London, whose growth seems to be gaining momentum, with thirty–two congregations planted in a fifteen year period, our present experience is that the more we continue, the harder it is to expand. This team has found growth much slower. One reason may be the most difficult area being targeted. But the main reason is that our churches are getting too close to each other. We need to burst out of our Anglican parish boundaries. If we were free to do this and plant in neighbouring towns, I am confident that we could again double our congregation size, but we are definitely constricted in our growth by these artificial restraints. While recognising some pastoral and administrative benefits in the parish system, I long for the day when the Church of

England will move from maintenance to mission and suspend them, at least for an experimental period.

In the meantime, we battle on, aware of the fragile and tiny significance of our work compared to the continuing indifference of our community. None of the above gains has been made without sweat and tears. But we fight on, doing everything we can to gain new territory for the Kingdom of God. We continue to pray and plan in the light of the following quotation from Eileen Vincent, with which I conclude: 'It seems that if a work is to continue to grow rather than to "consolidate" (a word not found in my Bible!) the people need to be progressively taken forward from goal to goal. Once a target is attained – a building filled, new housegroups established – it is time to move on, time to present the next challenge. Too easily we stand still and pat ourselves on the back; before long we are losing ground.'

Charlie Cleverly

Appendix G
The Dilemma Facing a Growing Church

A brief survey of St Nicholas Nottingham, 1973–1991

Background

St Nicholas' Church, Nottingham, was built in a quiet backwater of the city. Three hundred years ago, when the present building was erected, it was surrounded by cottages and cobbled streets. Those cottages have long since been demolished to be replaced by red-brick factories, a modern pedestrian shopping precinct and the city's inner by-pass – described by some as 'the ugliest road in Europe'. The church now stands in splendid isolation on an island formed by a network of busy roads, fast-moving traffic, multi-storey car parks, high-rise office blocks, pubs and the shopping precinct. There are now no houses in the parish.

When I was appointed to the church as rector in 1973, the once-thriving congregation was dwindling fast. There were three services each Sunday which drew, between them, between 100–200 adults and a handful of children. Leaders in the church warned us not to expect growth. The balcony had only been occupied once, they told my wife and me on our first visit. 'That was when David

Sheppard, who was playing for England at Trent Bridge, had preached one Sunday.

But the church did grow. Within the first year of our time in Nottingham, students from the University and the Polytechnic attached themselves to the church and injected the somewhat dispirited congregation with new life. A little later, as renewal made its impact on our worship and life together, others were attracted to the church. Some were new to the city, some came from other churches, many came because they were brought by their friends, found faith and stayed. Further growth took place because many of the students, when they graduated, stayed in Nottingham and made their homes here.

The church, which looks comfortably full with 250 worshippers can hold 400 if five people squeeze into each pew and extra chairs are placed in the aisles. It was now beginning to seem quite full, and we experienced an exciting phase of the church's history.

Such growth brought not only joy and anticipation but inevitable problems. One was that we were losing what most people treasure about a church fellowship – a much-needed sense of belonging. We desperately needed to decentralise because of the unmanageable numbers.

At this stage of the church's history, core members of the congregation met together to listen to God. What we seemed to hear was that we were to give away what we had received. To go out. I suggested that one way to do this would be to divide the congregation. Some would continue to make St Nic's their base. Others – those who lived in a particular locality – should be encouraged to worship in a nearby church. I proposed that we should explore the possibility of church planting by 'manning' one of the many struggling Anglican churches in the diocese.

The proposal was met with dismay and disapproval

from a whole variety of sources. First, the PCC of St Nicholas' cautioned me. Such suggestions were inappropriate for two reasons, they claimed. The diocese would never approve and it would be seen as 'empire building'. It was several years before I took the matter further and, in the event, in the initial stages, the diocese did approve. When, in the early '80s, I mentioned this idea to the then archdeacon and the then bishop, I met, not with disapproval but with co-operation and support. In fact, we began to make progress. Two nearly redundant churches were looked at.

It was at this stage that we met further opposition. This time resistance came from the patrons – even though one of the named churches shared the same patrons as St Nic's. Further opposition came from the tiny residual congregation in the churches concerned. They did not want to be 'taken over'. Others in the diocese resisted from fear: 'We don't want two churches like St Nic's in the city,' they protested. But the main problem was the intractible system in which we are all trapped, as David Pytches has so rightly pointed out. To my sorrow, we reached the stalemate which still exists today. Senior diocesan staff expressed sadness too and, though I appreciated their support and recognise that they are extremely busy people with more to think about than church planting, I would have liked to have seen them act with greater courage and conviction despite the constrictions of the system.

Some results of failure to church-plant

The deadlock resulted in a gradual slump in numbers. This was to be expected. It is a well-documented fact that when a church becomes too full growth stops and decline sets in. The congregation had now peaked at over 700 adult worshippers per Sunday. The next five years saw them go down to 520.

The decline happened for a number of reasons. One was frustration. Another was disappointment. Another was bewilderment on the part of the members of the church who were aware of the negotiations which were taking place and who could not understand the bureaucracy which seemed to be obstructing rather than promoting the growth of the Kingdom of God. Hopes had been raised. The church had, to use David Pytches' language, been training its NCOs. It was now armed with well over 200 people eager for action but with nowhere to expand in their ministries.

Another result was a more practical one. The church was uncomfortably full. More than the optimum 400 people regularly attended the evening service and, on special occasions, like Guest Services, Carol Services and Confirmation Services, more than 600 adults packed themselves into the pews or spilled over to sit on the chancel carpet or the stone floor of the aisles.

Creative counteraction

When negotiations broke down – not once but several times – with all that that involved emotionally in terms of raised and dashed hopes – we began to look for other ways of giving away what we had been given so generously by God.

One method that was suggested was that we should continue to 'lend' groups of people to other churches in the city. The hope and expectation was that the bonds between the individuals concerned would so blossom with the incumbent and members of the congregation that, eventually, a permanent transfer would take place. Sadly, this did not happen. One reason was that, once again, the congregations concerned felt threatened by the in-coming group even though they worked hard to establish trust and rapport. At this time my wife and I were finding that we were being invited to speak at a variety of conferences in this country and abroad. The PCC, recognising that this was one way in which the Church could reach out to others, generously gave me ten or more weeks' absence per year from the parish to free me to develop this wider ministry. Our intention was to take teams with us. At first, we did this but found that busy parishioners who hold down responsible jobs and have growing families could not cope with the travelling, the time away from home and the demands of such ministry. Some of them suffered from burn-out and, looking back, I now see that it was detrimental to the life of the fellowship and to my leadership of it for me to have been away for so many weeks of the year – sometimes for long periods. What we had experimented with, clearly, was not a satisfactory solution to the problem.

Other key members of the church, like the evangelist J. John, the *Footprints Theatre Company*, and some of our musicians were also going out to other churches and fellowships, sometimes taking teams with them. Many of these visits clearly produced fruit for the Kingdom but this 'hit and run' ministry was very different from the kind of friendship, neighbourhood evangelism we had envisaged. This would have been more feasible for the people we had trained in the hope that they could serve the church within the community of which they were already a part.

Over the years, several members of our fellowship have left in dribs and drabs. Some have felt called to support their local church. Others have left from frustration and have sought to play their part in serving other, smaller, struggling churches. Many of these have found it difficult to settle and, after a prolonged and painful period of adjustment, have eventually returned or moved on to yet other fellowships. Some have been lost to the Church of

England altogether. David Pytches mentions many of the
reasons for this tragic state of affairs. One of the chief
reasons, as I see it from our experience here in Nottingham, is that such gifted, highly motivated people need to
work with leadership structures which have been
touched by the renewal. They need to work with a clergyman who welcomes genuine open partnership with lay
leaders, who encourages a widely-shared leadership, and
who seeks to follow the living Christ, rather than to
pacify, pander or keep peace at all costs. In the absence of
such support, the most resilient, trained NCO is rendered
ineffective and grows discouraged.

The options

Since to date, our longing to church plant is still
thwarted, as I see it, there are three possible options still
open to us. One is to enlarge the building, another is to
opt for multi-congregations (like St Thomas', Crookes,
Sheffield), the third is still to seek ways to give away our
growth.

Alas, although St Nic's is surrounded by a large
churchyard, extension of the premises is not possible. St
Nic's is a listed building and no extension of the building
is permitted. Hampered by yet another piece of bureaucracy, we are still seeking to be creative by redesigning
the interior of the building. By erecting a second balcony
we can increase the seating capacity by about 15 per cent.
This falls a long way short of the much needed 50 per cent
increase. But even if we could enlarge that much, the
question still needs to be asked whether it would be right
to draw even more people away from their locality to a
city centre location to worship?

Multi-congregations would also pose problems. If we
choose this option, it will entail the addition of a further
evening service – say at 9.00 pm like St Thomas'. The

morning service would also need to divide and the already fragmented fellowship would be further fragmented. At present the two congregations overlap sufficiently to enable one sub-structure of fellowship groups to serve both congregations. Unity is just possible. With the move to four congregations each would surely take on a very distinct identity and need its own group sub-structure.

If, like St Thomas', St Nic's occupied a prime position in a large residential parish, it might make good sense to increase the number of services. As I have already explained, that is not our situation. Some of our members travel several miles to reach us. If we were to have four congregations, each with its own fellowship group network, then we could face the distinct farcical possibility of four St Nic's house groups meeting in the same road three miles from the church but not knowing each other. Surely this is not the way forward? There must be a better answer.

This persuades me and the leaders of the church, that the call which came to us so many years ago, to go out, giving away the growth we have enjoyed, is still the best, indeed, the only real way forward. That is one reason why, when I read the proof copy of this timely book, I thanked God that, at last, someone in their position was willing to speak out against the anomalies which are hindering rather than advancing the growth of the Kingdom of God in our country. What we, at St Nic's long for is what he describes in this book: the support of the diocese to plant churches, not to 'empire build' for ourselves but to create a caring community which brings glory to Christ; a community which will be a delight to worship in and which will serve and revive some of the beautiful churches of our land which are in danger of closure for lack of support.

The present

Meanwhile, it seems, we must continue to wait. But we refuse to stagnate. So three years ago we turned another corner.

The twenty-four church house groups were formed into six regional groups – like mini-congregations. Each regional group was encouraged to meet fortnightly in some suitable church or hall in their particular suburb of the city. The local vicar's consent was sought before the group was set up and such was the level of co-operation that one group actually meets in another Anglican church. In these groups, individuals continue to develop leadership skills and to gain the experience of being a little more than 'NCOs'. If church planting ever becomes a possibility, they are prepared, at the ready. If not, we trust that the experience will bear fruit for the Kingdom in some other way or some other place in the years to come.

We continue to work for growth. As I put it to members of the church at the Annual General Meeting in April 1990, we have set ourselves the target, during the first four years of the decade of evangelism, of 10 per cent growth per year so that, to quote from the document, 'By December 1993, we work for growth in our congregation, say by 40%, so that by 1994 church planting can begin!'

Because of the background I have outlined, this vision has met with a mixed response. Morale is not high, though church attendance figures show that church growth is currently on target. Many, unnerved by the experiences I have described, and aware that the rigid parochial system places huge obstacles in the way of church planting, fear that it will never happen. It is difficult to work for a goal you suspect might be vetoed at any stage. Yet what other option is there? The multi-congregation option remains a second-best alternative. But for the moment the vision document is clear. Excited by the church planting we have witnessed in other parts of the Anglican Communion, like in Singapore, we want to continue to press for church planting here in our own country, here in our own city of Nottingham, which we have learned to love for Christ.

David Huggett 14.1.91

Bibliography

Avis, Paul, *Anglicanism and the Christian Church*, Edinburgh, T & T Clark, 1989

Barlow, Frank, *The English Church 1066–1154*, Longman, London, 1979

Bunting, Ian D, *Claiming the Urban Village*, Grove Booklet No 6, 1989

Cleverley, Charles, *Church Planting*, Scripture Union, 1991

Gibbs, Eddie, *Ten Growing Churches*, MARC Europe, Bromley, 1984

Hargreaves, Alan, *The Case for Lay Presidency*, Grove Booklet, 1990

Hopkins, Bob, *Church Planting: Models for Mission in the Church of England*, Grove Booklets (Nos 4 & 8)

Moltmann, Jürgen, *The Church in the Power of the Holy Spirit*, SCM, 1979

Nott, Peter, *Moving Forward: A Strategy for the Diocese of Norwich*, 1989

Tiller, John, *A Strategy for the Church's Ministry*, ACCM 1983

Warren, Robert, *On the Anvil*, Highland, 1990

White, John, *When the Spirit Comes with Power*, Hodder & Stoughton, 1990

Wimber, John, *Power Evangelism*, Hodder & Stoughton, 1985

A Short History of St John's, Downshire Hill, Hampstead (published privately)

Faith in the City, Churchman Press (distributed by Balley Bros & Swissen)

Lambeth Report, 1988, Anglican Consultative Council

Plan for Evangelism and Church Growth in the Diocese of Wellington, New Zealand, 1988

The Canons of the Church of England, promulgated by the Convocations of Canterbury and York in 1964 and 1969

The Case for Regional Episcopacy, Diocese of Chile, Bolivia and Peru, 1968

The Church Times, London, May 1990

The Church of England Newspaper, London, January 26, 1990